Poet *to* Poet

i.m. Professor D.G. Kendall
mathematician, and sometime astronomer and poet,
1918-2007

Poet *to* Poet

Edward Thomas's letters to Walter de la Mare

Edited with an Introduction
by Judy Kendall

Transcriber's Preface by Piers Pennington

SEREN

Seren is the book imprint of
Poetry Wales Press Ltd
Nolton Street, Bridgend, Wales

www.serenbooks.com
facebook.com/serenbooks
Twitter: @SerenBooks

Selection and editorial matter © Judy Kendall, 2012
Transcriber's Preface © Piers Pennington, 2012

The right of Judy Kendall to be identified
as the Editor of this Work has been asserted
in accordance with the Copyright, Designs
and Patents Act, 1988.

ISBN 978-1-85411-580-5

A CIP record for this title is available from
the British Library

The publisher works with the financial assistance
of the Welsh Books Council

Cover photograph of Edward Thomas by kind permission of the Estate of
Edward Thomas and Special Collections, Cardiff University Library

Printed by the CPI Group (UK) Ltd, Croydon

Contents

A Seventeenth Century Icon

With a bold stroke,
Under the yoke,
In words of colour Demetrios spoke.
His world did not glow with that radiant light:
Nothing shone then but a glimmering flame,
Hope-kindled, heart-cradled through life's long night.
Now dawn has come, and all men admire
The icon that tells us Demetrios' name,
Embellished with gold, emblazoned with fire
For those who can read what his colours proclaim.

DGK

Introduction

We wish you were at the other corner of the triangle, & that
an equilateral one.

(Thomas to de la Mare, Herefordshire, August 1914,
where Thomas and Frost were staying with their families)

On an envelope of a letter containing Edward Thomas's almost
overwhelmingly enthusiastic reception of *Peacock Pie*, Walter
de la Mare writes the words "very special, precious". This is an apt
description of the two hundred and fifty or so letters Thomas
writes to de la Mare, carefully preserved in an album in Oxford
University's Bodleian Library, purchased from the de la Mare
family in 1976.

The correspondence ranges from 1906 to 1917. A few letters
and cards detail arrangements to meet in town. Others discuss
possibilities of walks and the sharing of writing retreats. A number
lay out the mechanics of making a living through writing. Several
reflect the intimacy that developed between their two families, with
de la Mare and his family regularly spending a month's holiday in
a cottage a four or five mile walk from Thomas's place. And many
bear witness to the tenderness between the two men as they
provided mutual support during periods of depression and physical ill health. Comments like "I wish you were nearer" crop up
throughout. There are tantalising glimpses of their daily writing
practices, details of their writing careers and discussion of specific
pieces of writing, sometimes right down to particular pages and
lines.

The letters are touching, gentle and heart-searching. They open
a window into the lives and thoughts of two highly talented poets
and offer an opportunity to witness the magic, mystery, and sensitive openness with which they both lived. As an entirety, they
create a special space. It is a privilege to eavesdrop on these two
writers' honest and sometimes difficult conversations. And it is
eavesdropping. De la Mare may have preserved the letters he
received from Thomas with care, but none of his letters to Thomas
survive, because Thomas burnt his side of the correspondence. So

it is not only with delight but with temerity and humility that these sometimes nakedly honest scripts need to be read.

A sense of poignancy is unavoidable. While de la Mare's star rises, Thomas's appears to drop. De la Mare is still making his way as a poet and critic when the two men first meet. His respect for Thomas as a writer is evident. He seeks his advice, sending him poem drafts, and receiving detailed comment. However, by 1909, de la Mare is discussing Thomas's critical writings on an equal basis, and helping Thomas with his proofs of the 1910 poetic essays, *Rest and Unrest*. De la Mare's rising confidence is matched by public recognition. In 1908, a Civil List pension allows him to leave his City job and devote himself to writing. The *Times Literary Supplement* and *Saturday Westminster Gazette* employ him as a regular reviewer. He is given a lifelong subscription to the London Library, a boon he shares with Thomas. In 1911, he begins work as a publisher's reader for Heinemann and his adult novel *The Return* wins the coveted Polignac Prize. In 1912, he is invited to write quarterly articles for *Edinburgh Review*, and is included in the first Georgian anthology *Georgian Poetry 1911-12*, as he is in all the subsequent *Georgian Poetry* anthologies. He takes on the Royal Society of Literature Chair of Fiction in 1915, and in the same year is named as a beneficiary of Rupert Brooke's sale of writings. These soon become a significant source of income, and result in an American lecture tour in 1916.

Meanwhile, Thomas watches his own reviewing fall away, and his books gradually earn less money. His setbacks coincide with de la Mare's achievements so often that he must have grimaced. De la Mare gains grants where Thomas is refused. De la Mare moves to more spacious housing while Thomas downsizes for reasons of economy. De la Mare gives up some of his more onerous review-ing work, which Thomas, struggling financially, asks if he can take on. De la Mare writes the poetry that Thomas feels he himself, as "only a reviewer" cannot. De la Mare is invited into the *Georgian Poetry* anthologies in which Thomas never appears. De la Mare lectures in England and America after Thomas has baulked at similar opportunities.

These contrasts must have been all the more galling given the initial positions of the two men. In 1906, Arthur Ransome describes Thomas in a March 1907 *Bookman* full-length 'Gallery' feature as "one of the best critics and most delightful country essayists we possess". De la Mare's own 'Gallery' feature as poet, written by Thomas, does not appear till December 1910, Thomas picturing him as "airily but securely perched on a single tower whose foundation is English literature and his own personality in the proportion of one to three."

Neat a reading as this might be, it would be grossly inaccurate to suggest that de la Mare's meteoric rise mirrors and even effects a demonic fall for Thomas. On the contrary, close reading of Thomas's letters show how changes in de la Mare's life, and in particular the liberation to pursue the writing he most wishes to do, inspire Thomas. When de la Mare hands in his notice to Anglo-American Oil in 1908, Thomas leaves the Royal Commission on Ancient Monuments in Wales and Monmouthshire, a job he dislikes. The consequent prodigious creative output that de la Mare experiences is matched by Thomas who produces the poetic sketches that later become *Rest and Unrest*. There are good grounds for arguing that de la Mare's development as a poet, which, as the letters show, clearly delights Thomas, has strong bearings on Thomas's growing confidence in his own writing abilities and eventual movement into verse.

It is also worth bearing in mind that de la Mare's success as a poet is more than matched by Thomas's output of books, however financially draining he may have found them. In 1910 Thomas is working on *Feminine Influence on the Poets*, as well as preparing for *Maeterlinck*, and *The Icknield Way*. In 1911 he takes on *Lafcadio Hearn*, *Celtic Stories* and *The Isle of Wight*, and also starts to plan *Swinburne* and *Walter Pater*. 1912 sees him working on these, together with *George Borrow* and *The Country*.

The depth of Thomas's appreciation of de la Mare's work is evident in the fact that, despite the divergence in their fortunes, he continues to champion de la Mare's particular gifts as a writer. Although his very early reviews of de la Mare's *Songs of Childhood* and *Henry Brocken* are somewhat lukewarm, from 1906 on he becomes one of de la Mare's strongest supporters. He entitles his 9 November 1906 *Daily Chronicle* review of de la Mare's *Poems*, 'A New Voice in Poetry', taking the opportunity to revise publicly his opinion of *Songs of Childhood*, which he now calls an "almost transparent lyric stream". He asks de la Mare if he can include his work in *The Pocket Book of Poems and Songs for the Open Air*, telling his co-anthologist and writer-friend, the poet and playwright,

Gordon Bottomley, in July 1906 that "I regret that I saw nothing in any [of de la Mare's poems] except the nonsense pieces in 1902, while I now see that it is poetry". He writes feelingly of de la Mare's fantastical novel in the December 1910 *Bookman*: "It is difficult to be moderate in speaking of 'The Three Mulla-Mulgars', it is so singular and so beautiful." He fêtes de la Mare's 1912 poetry collection *The Listeners*, declaring to him in June 1913 (letter number 177) that "[W.H.] Hudson's are the only other living man's books that give me such perfect pleasure, with its edge perhaps a little keener for the faintest taint of envy". His unbridled delight and joy in *Peacock Pie* comes through both in his reviews and his letters, his September 1913 *Bookman* review recording how "I am continually putting in my thumb, pulling out a plum".

This respect for de la Mare continues during difficult times. Thomas might write to Bottomley on 31 October 1912 that de la Mare is "a too busy man now, reading for Heinemann & reviewing multifariously & never quite unpuckering in our scanty meetings", but he remains very appreciative of de la Mare's 'Longlegs'. This poem is a loving homage to Thomas. The story goes that as Thomas was cycling around the countryside on one of his research trips, a small boy yelled after him the country name for a crane fly, 'Longlegs'. Thomas responds happily to de la Mare's poem: signing himself 'Longlegs' in an 8 May 1910 letter (70), and, on publication of the poem in *Peacock Pie* in 1913, ending a June 1913 letter (177) with a call from the poem, 'Cooee'. In 1912, he dedicates *Swinburne* to de la Mare, and continues to look out for him, alerting him to reviewing and poem publication possibilities. At the end of March 1913, on Thomas's urging, they even coincide at Dillybrook Farm in Wiltshire, one of Thomas's regular writing retreats.

Perhaps one reason that this writerly friendship survives is the fact that although Thomas has difficulties in finding a market for his work during the period of their friendship, he is also aware of his own growing confidence and daring as a writer. A 14 December 1909 letter to Bottomley laments: "By comparison with others that I know – like de la Mare – I seem essentially like the other men in the train & I should like not to be." However, in later letters, as his poetry begins to pour out, Thomas changes his perspective on himself, appearing more and more resilient to adverse criticism particularly of his poetry, and surer and surer of his own intents and effects.

As early as September 1913, at the end of his essay 'Insomnia', published in *The Last Sheaf*, and in a letter to de la Mare written on the seventh of September (187), Thomas records an attempt at poetry. These accounts of writing a poem are highly interesting to any student of the composing process. They detail the effect on poetic composition of the poet's simultaneous awareness of his environment and physical sensations. 'Insomnia' examines the factors that hinder creative composition and looks at the dangers concomitant with too much attention on process, emphasising the importance of a lack of direct focus. The letter to de la Mare subtly indicates where Thomas is moving in his own poetic work. By means of a slightly altered quotation from Pope, Thomas sets de la Mare in the dubious company of "the mob of gentlemen that rhyme with ease". This implies that Thomas has reservations about too habitual a facility with rhyme. It also contrasts with the very loose manipulation of rhyme in his own subsequent poetry in which delighted divergence from fixed rhyme schemes is accompanied by daring combinations of metrical and speech rhythms.

The two poets' experiences of composition coincide in curious ways. In late 1914, de la Mare is laid up with appendicitis. His writing blossoms as he scribbles rhymes for a book to be illustrated by Ralph Hodgson, which in fact never materializes. "He goes on all day, covering sheets of paper with that small weird writing" writes Henry Newbolt to Alice Hylton on 20 January 1915. Also in late 1914, enforced leisure due to lack of reviewing work frees Thomas up creatively. In a 24 October 1914 letter to the publisher's reader Edward Garnett, he writes: "I get scraps of work, very few, & plenty of time to write what I like & find I can write." He experiences an extraordinary run of poetic creativity, producing sometimes as many as three poems a day. Shortly afterwards, due to a sprained ankle, he, like de la Mare, is confined physically, and in the space of two months composes thirty three poems.

Although *Feminine Influence on the Poets* is Thomas's only book to deal with the subject of poetic composition head on, he addresses it frequently elsewhere. *Swinburne* explores the relations between words and rhythm. The preface to *The Icknield Way* reveals interest in the lack of a perceived beginning or end to the

composing process. A 31 December 1911 letter (125) to de la
Mare shows Thomas making use of research on Pater to develop
ideas on the relations between writing and speech, a train of
thought later blossoming in his poetry after his 1914 discussions
with Robert Frost.

When writing of Mary Coleridge's poems in the February 1908
Bookman, Thomas uses terms that foreshadow his later experiments in verse. She has a "resolute delicacy, an ardent quietness,
a frank reserve", while her rhythms "abound in originality, and are
never mere lengths of syllables". Similarly, the letters to de la Mare
reveal an undercurrent of fascination with rhythm, syllable length
and improvisation, as well as a strong interest in dreams, in
conscious and unconscious perceptions, and in the view of the
child.

The two men exchange creative ideas, and, at least once, they
agree to write stories on the same topic: time. Thomas's story,
'The time deposit', is published in 1911 in *The Nation*, and
reprinted in *Cloud Castle* in 1922 as 'Saved time'. De la Mare's
'The Vats', eventually written in 1917, is published in *The Riddle
and other stories* in 1923.

Their walks become sources of creativity. Thomas's 'The Stile',
in *Light and Twilight*, records a July walk with a friend, probably in
1909 or 1910. The two men talk

> easily and warmly together, in such a way that there was no
> knowing whose was any one thought, because we were in
> electrical contact and each leapt to complete the other's
> words, just as if some poet had chosen to use the form of
> an eclogue and had made us the two shepherds who were
> to utter his mind through our dialogue.

Thomas's 1916 poem, 'The sun used to shine', echoes 'The
Stile' in its depiction of the easy rhythms of intimate speech
reflected and reflecting the rhythms of two friends walking.
Although for Thomas, 'The sun used to shine' celebrates his
friendship with Frost, the resemblance to 'The Stile' suggests a
tacit acknowledgement of his earlier intimacies with writer-
friends, and in particular with de la Mare, to whom Helen Thomas
writes in the 1940s that "'The Stile' enshrines his feeling for you."

The two men show a similar interest in improvisation and the
fine line between spontaneity and intent. In a 19 November1907

letter (23) Thomas tells de la Mare that Herbert Trench is 'good' but one poem is 'a bit made up'. De la Mare's December 1907 *Bookman* review of Trench seems partly to reflect Thomas's comments on this poet: "here and there, in the volume, the roughness and looseness of phrase and metre seem almost an intentional blemish". Later, in the December 1910 *Bookman*, Thomas celebrates the spontaneous quality of de la Mare's *The Three Mulla-Mulgars*:

> Possibly the outline of a great part is due to improvisation, or a series of improvisations. It has the freshness, but no flimsiness or mere liveliness. The adventures grow out of one another as they might have grown in a happy and fruitful mind.

In March 1915 (237), de la Mare sees Thomas's poetry as having "gone wrong over metre", but by 1917 he comes to appreciate the merits of this looser use of metre, writing in the 18 October 1917 *Times Literary Supplement*:

> [I]t is as if a wind had suddenly come out of the south, setting the waters free. Thomas had been criticising other men's poetry for twenty years, and all these years had been steadily storing up his own. It is a poetry that not only breaks away from poetic convention, into a verse in which the rhymes are like the faintest of echoes, the metre at times scarcely distinguishable, and the form as insubstantial as a ghost's, but much of it is "about" what most poets leave unremarked, or, at any rate, unrecorded.

Non-logical ways of working are important to both writers. Although de la Mare continually redrafted his work, his method of writing poetry involving calculated use of word lists, he also relied on more intuitive approaches. Many of the poems he shares with Thomas were written around midnight after working all day as reader for Heinemann. Theresa Whistler reports in the chapter on *Peacock Pie* in her de la Mare biography that his recipe for writing them was "Get very tired first." Both men too, as their letters reveal, make use of dreams as creative sources of inspiration. Each entitles a poem 'A Dream'. They describe dreams to each other, valuing them as sources of creativity, as in Thomas's 29 March 1911 letter (99). Thomas's 1913 prose piece 'St Ann's Cottage', collected in *Cloud Castle*, explores a sequence of associatively linked images or 'wool-gathering'. Elsewhere, he works with his earliest experiences and memories, experimenting with writing methods in a pseudo-novel, an autobiography and an unfinished piece referred to by Thomas as a 'fiction'. The title of a chapter of his autobiographical novel, the 1913 *The Happy-go-lucky Morgans*, includes the word 'Wool-gathering' and he continues to wool-gather in much of that chapter and the rest of the book. Thomas discusses this method with de la Mare in an intriguing letter in early February 1913 (164). Glen Cavaliero has described Thomas's approach in the 1983 introduction to *The Happy-go-lucky Morgans* as "a technique of progression backwards and forwards that anticipates the work [...] of Ford Madox Ford and Virginia Woolf". It also reflects the work of Freud, and Thomas would have encountered Freud's theories about consciousness, sub-consciousness, dreams and emphasis on associative connections through the nervous disorder specialist and Jungian champion, Godwin Baynes, who was Thomas's doctor in 1912 and 1913.

De la Mare's 1 December 1910 *Times Literary Supplement* review of Thomas's *Feminine Influence on the Poets* indicates the importance that natural and almost haphazard movements of thought hold for both men. The book is

> a kind of delightful labyrinth through the refreshing, delusive, beckoning alleys of which we wander, now in the company of one poet, now of another, but always with the same guide talking and suggesting, but (though perhaps almost unconsciously) intent on one thing, that we shall never flatter ourselves that we have reached the centre, [...] [as] we are arrested and lured in a book that resembles a series of stepping stones which conduct us cautiously into the middle of a stream at flood, and leave us there

This value for spontaneity, and for a position that stays at least one step short of finality, is evident in Thomas's reservations in the December 1910 *Bookman* about de la Mare's use of blank verse and sonnets in *Poems*: "their rhythm does not suit Mr. de la Mare and makes him eloquent". He also repeatedly praises de la Mare's flowing rhythm and lack of self-conscious polish, qualities he aims to achieve for himself. When he responds to de la Mare's criticism of his mature poetry in the spring of 1915 (238), he stresses how if his poems are not 'chantable', they are at least 'speakable'.

Thomas's indebtedness to de la Mare in his own long journey from reviewer to poet is nowhere more strikingly acknowledged than in the many echoes his poems contain of de la Mare's verse. *Edward Thomas's Poets* has documented connections between twenty-five of de la Mare's and Thomas's poems, but there are more. These include Thomas's 'The Green Roads' and 'But these things also' which seem to echo de la Mare's 'Many A Mickle' from *Peacock Pie*; Thomas's 'The Owl' which chimes with de la Mare's 'The Mother Bird' from *Songs of Childhood*; and Thomas's 'Lob' which perhaps owes something to de la Mare's 'Lob Lie By The Fire' from *A Child's Day: A Book of Rhymes*.

Virginia Woolf reviewed both Thomas and de la Mare in the 1917 and 1918 *Times Literary Supplement*. Her 11 October 1917 *Times Literary Supplement* review of Thomas's *Literary Pilgrims in England* celebrates the "individual quality of the [book's] pilgrimage" through counties and poets "connected on the most elastic and human principle". For her, *Literary Pilgrims* is "like the talk of a very good talker":

> We have seldom read a book indeed which gives a better feeling of England than this one. Never perfunctory or conventional, but always saying what strikes him as the true or interesting or characteristic thing, Mr. Thomas brings the very look of the fields and roads before us; he brings the poets too; and no one will finish the book without a sense that he [sic] knows and respects the author.

Her 30 August 1918 review of de la Mare's *Motley and Other Poems* recollects an earlier exposure to de la Mare's work and "the shock of surprise with which we encountered this sharply and, considering its surroundings, almost improperly individual voice". She documents how "surprise, the sense of finding an unseized emotion reduced to its unmistakable form of words, possesses us", and evokes his extraordinary ability with sound, and silence, in words that could well apply to the correspondence between de la Mare and Thomas: "The poem ends, in silence and hush, but, strangely, the sound goes on. The quiet has become full of tremors and vibrations: we are still listening long after the words are done."

Judy Kendall, November 2010

Transcriber's Preface

It may seem strange to point out that the letters presented in this book are not the letters which have been collected into the large blue album lodged in the Bodleian Library. But for all the manifold gains of transcription and publication, much of the original nuance has unavoidably been lost: Thomas's sentences are now shaped by the conventions of the printed page, the variations of his handwriting flattened into the fixity of type. Indeed, to read the letters as gathered in the album is to realise that although much of their individual meaning is communicated by their content, collectively their materiality tells at least some of the story. There are, to begin with, the sheets of notepaper and the lettercards on which the correspondence is for the most part conducted, many of the sheets and a number of the lettercards displaying addresses printed at their heads. There are then the smaller postcards for briefer messages, introduced once the friends have become more familiar, and often used to arrange meetings, a number of these again displaying printed addresses. Interspersed throughout, and contrasting with such propriety, are letters which seem to have been written more impulsively, on whatever suitable paper was at hand. Then, as the correspondence approaches its end, pencil gradually replaces the usual pen as Thomas, having enlisted, writes to de la Mare from Hare Hall and a number of other camps. Finally, there are the few pages sent from the fields of France, the scrawling hand seeking to make the most of its limited space in the most uncertain of circumstances.

While some of the letters suggest their writing to be a welcome respite from more pressing concerns, Thomas from the very beginning was often a hasty correspondent, and the characteristics of his handwriting confirm this to be the case. He seems to acknowledge the frequent difficulty of its reading in the letter dated 14 October 1909 (letter number 62 below): "I got a prize for handwriting when I was 13, so there", he playfully begins, with what sounds like a trumping riposte to a criticism levelled by de la Mare. Many difficult words are made clear by the local context of the sentence in question, others by broader reference to personal and contemporary knowledge, but, however practised the eye, only with time do some of the markings on the page resolve into a word, if at all – with a very few remaining finally indecipherable, here. "Even to one that knows it well, the names / Half decorate, half perplex, the thing it is", Thomas meditated in the early poem 'Old Man', and such a relation between name and thing approaches the relation in manuscripts between a word's particular iteration on the page and the mind's abstracted understanding, the former decorating and, at times, perplexing the latter. This may seem to be reading too much into the accidentals of momentary and spontaneous formation, but the largely quotidian nature of the correspondence offers a fascinating chance to observe the workaday manifestation of Thomas's hand. The letter which introduces the two men looks almost like a fair copy, Thomas being keen to make a good impression upon a stranger whose poems he admires and wishes to use in an anthology, the hand small and fine, making no mistakes; but in the following letters, which establish the friendship, no attempt is made to disguise the sometimes messy reality of writing by hand: words are retrospectively added, words and even whole sentences are crossed through (this happening as early as the fourth letter), and, less conspicuously, letters beginning abandoned words are overwritten by sentences which stand in their stead – overwriting also often doing the work of correction. Such changes of direction are strong reminders of just how dynamic is the relation between writing and thinking; and for a writer estimated to have penned more than a million words over the course of his lifetime, so many waking hours would have been spent at the desk that it is tempting to read the movements of the hand as being deeply at one with, and occasionally prevailing over, those of the mind.

P.J. Croft, in his revelatory *Autograph Poetry in the English Language*, introduces a facsimile of the poem 'Rain', written as Thomas was 'coming home' from Hare Hall Camp, with a description which holds true for the letters:

> The speed of Thomas's handwriting is reflected in many features: the occasional joining of words, the extempore shortenings of individual forms (*a, g,* etc.), the variable treatment of *i* (sometimes left undotted, sometimes dotted over the stem but more often at varying distances to the right) and *t* (sometimes uncrossed, sometimes crossed

through the stem, the cross-stroke sometimes begun far to
the right and often run on into a following letter whether in
the same word or at the start of the next). Another conspicuous feature is the highly flexible spacing, both within and
between words.

If the manuscript of the poem displays only the occasional
joining of words, then the frequency of the ligatures throughout
the letters is one of their defining features: not only is it rare to find
a letter in which two words are not joined together, but sometimes
three or even four words are connected in this way. An intensifica-
tion of the practice of cursive handwriting, it is a habit of
economy, one which minimises movement and saves time: in the
letter dated 27 June 1912 (143), and the words 'at the very end',
for instance, the 't's in 'at' and 'the' are both crossed by a retro-
spective stroke which then becomes the 'v' beginning 'very end',
the pen working through the two words in a single movement
before leaving the page on the downstroke of 'n', to draw an
isolated 'd'. There are also more curious instances, however, as
with the words 'It turned out so fine today', which begin the letter
dated 'Sunday evening' (170). In the pen's first movement, the
stem of the 't' which ends 'out' runs into the 's' of 'so', the second
movement returning to cross the 't' before becoming the 'f' of
'fine', there being two lines of connection in the space between
'out' and 'so' as a result. The highly flexible spacing is also much
in evidence, but this is most notable between words rather than
within them, and often when they are separated by a point of
punctuation. A number of Thomas's commas and full stops are
not anchored against the words they follow but are instead delayed
and allowed to float in the space between words – sometimes
closer to the word just gone, sometimes in the middle of the two,
and sometimes closer to the word to come – as if the space is
positively signifying the time taken to decide a sentence's direction: whether it will end, whether it will pause, or whether it will be
continued with one of the plus signs which Thomas often uses in
place of the word 'and'. His approach to dashes is also highly
suggestive in this regard. In the main these are used convention-
ally, to indicate parentheses or to link separate parts of a sentence,
but sometimes they can be more ambiguous: in shorter letters
which are not broken into paragraphs, the insertion of a dash
between completed sentences suggests an equivalent shift in sense,

while in other instances they seem again to be recording the passing of time, and, with it, the mind's deliberation – inverting yet also complementing the spaces.

These features are all to be found in the letter dated 20 April 1911 (103, reproduced on p. 20). Thomas was by this time alternating between Wick Green and Rusham Road, but this letter is written on the reverse of an outdated sheet of notepaper from a former address (Berryfield Cottage, Ashfield, Petersfield), which has been torn in half, most likely. There are many ligatures: in the second line of the address, and, then, in the letter's first (though here the 'f' is not fully crossed, another indication of haste), second, fifth, sixth, seventh, eighth, ninth (the 't' here again not being fully crossed), eleventh, twelfth, and fourteenth lines – and, as well as this, the pen makes no pause for the apostrophes in 'wife's' (line 3) and 'don't' (line 12). There are also more obvious indications that the letter's writing has been rushed: not only are the words 'I would' crossed through in the ninth line, and the word 'this' inserted as an afterthought in the seventh, but 'at' in the sixth line overwrites the beginning of an abandoned thought, possibly correcting it. There are some unusual spacings, too: the full stop in the second line, between 'astray' and 'It', like the full stop in the tenth line, between 'Tuesday' and 'I', and the plus sign between 'you' and 'think' in the eleventh, is long delayed, being closer to the following word than the preceding one. And then there is the dash at the letter's end, which introduces a disconsolate confidence while also intimating Thomas's reluctance to be doing so.

As in the famous poem by John Keats – which Thomas briefly mentions in his book on Keats and wryly echoes in his poem, 'The long small room' – these letters to Walter de la Mare reveal "This living hand, now warm and capable".

                                                             Piers Pennington

13 Rusham Rd
Balham SW.

20 IV 11

My dear de la Mare

Thanks for your note. I hope mine to you got astray. It was enclosed in one of my wife's to yours, & informed you that I was here & hereabouts for a few days. As you will be sending Dick off tomorrow & probably by the 3.45 — can't we meet at the station & then go & have tea? Let me know this, & let my wife know the train to meet. But in case tomorrow's tea is inconvenient to you we will meet on Tuesday. I should very much like to come home with you, & think I will if you don't decide against me on such an occasion. — I am here working & for the purpose of seeing my family & myself.

Yours ever
E.T.

Thomas's letter of 20 April 1911 (103)

A Note on the Text

The letters as they appear in this book have been shaped by editorial decisions made during their transcription and preparation for publication. The aim throughout has been to present a reading text geared towards fluency of content rather than close accuracy of transcription. No attempt has been made to reproduce exactly the spacing in the sentences nor the ligatures between words, although the headnotes point out and describe instances of particular interest. Similarly, no attempt has been made to reproduce the varying lengths of dashes; shorter dashes have been indicated by one em dash, longer dashes by two em dashes run together. The plus signs which Thomas uses in place of 'and' are indicated by ampersands. Crossings out and overwritings have generally been elided, to present Thomas's final thought, but occasional examples of interest are discussed in the headnotes or retained in the text. Mistakes in Thomas's spelling have not been corrected. Conjectures of words difficult to determine are followed by a question mark and enclosed in square brackets; those which are indecipherable are indicated by a question mark alone, enclosed in square brackets. The varying indentations marking the beginnings of paragraphs have all been standardised by a regular space. Addresses printed or written variously to the right of the page now begin at the same point, while those printed or written generally in the centre of the page have here been centred. Archivists or librarians have often suggested dates in pencil, and these words are transcribed in square brackets. A few headnotes point out whether or not a letter has been written on a sheet of notepaper, but this is not maintained throughout the book. Capitalised addresses tend to be an indication of headed notepaper. Distinctions between letters, lettercards, and postcards are not noted, although again some of the headnotes provide this information.

In the Bodleian album, the letters are mainly placed chronologically, although there are a few anomalies, and some undated letters at the end. If a letter runs to more than one page then it has more than one folio number. Some letters have been misplaced or misdated. In a January 1914 letter, for example, Thomas has written 1913. Where appropriate, *Poet to Poet* has adjusted the order of letters, using content and context to ascertain dates. Two letters that still cannot be dated are included at the end, a remaining mystery for the reader to unravel. A guide to correspondence between folio and letter number can be found in the appendix.

Longlegs

To E.T.

Longlegs – he yelled 'Coo-ee!'
       And all across the combe
Shrill and shrill it sang – rang through
       The clear green gloom
Fairies there were a-spinning,
       And a white tree-maid
Lifted her eyes, and listened
       In her rain-sweet glade.
Bunnie to bunnie stamped; old Wat
       Chin-deep in bracken sate;
A throstle piped, 'I'm by, I'm by!'
       Clear to his timid mate.
And there was Longlegs straddling,
       And hearkening was he,
To distant Echo thrilling back
       A thin 'Coo-ee!'

A note by Walter de la Mare written late in life quoted in chapter eight of *The Life of Walter de la Mare* by Theresa Whistler

Most writers – and probably most painters and musicians – would, I think, agree that its most fortunate, a poem, (or a story or a picture) brings its plan with it. Its what and how are part and parcel of itself. The bubble (out of the sediment) resembles a cocoon – a bit odd! But it takes endless pains and labour in the unwinding; and the thread may snap. Fortunately we only so much control our own minds as we do our bodies. Best to let them work in their own way, and trust to Providence. But keep at it.

Letters from Edward Thomas
to Walter de la Mare

Section I
1906-1910 The Critic and the Poet

Before the two poets make contact, Thomas is already highly respected as a critic and writer of 'country books', as listed in his third letter to de la Mare, while de la Mare has published a collection of poems, *Songs of Childhood*, under the pseudonym, Ramal in 1902, a novel, *Henry Brocken*, in 1904, and a second poetry collection, *Poems*, in 1906. He has also been writing signed articles for the *Bookman* since 1905, with Thomas joining him as a fellow *Bookman* critic in 1906.

The letters from 1906 to 1910 start with Thomas approaching de la Mare for permission to include his poems in *The Pocket Book of Poems and Songs for the Open Air*, and de la Mare seeking a greater acquaintance with Thomas, renowned poetry critic and reviewer of his work. As the letters continue, Thomas makes efforts to cement this relationship further, and the two men and their families become close, Thomas commenting on de la Mare's and his friend John Freeman's poetry, and advising de la Mare in his journey from poet to reviewer and critic.

1

The anthology is The Pocket Book of Poems and Songs for the Open Air. *In a 1 January 1907 letter to his clergyman friend Jesse Berridge Thomas, reveals that the poems in this volume are chosen in order not 'to clash with other anthologists'. Hence his eagerness to include de la Mare, a relatively unknown poet.*

Walter de la Mare Esq.,   THE   WEALD,
c/o Messrs Longmans, Green & Co..   Nr. SEVENOAKS

Dear Sir,
    I am making an anthology of poems for the open air and should be very sorry not to include at least one of yours. May I use one or two of the following? —
    'The Child in the Story awakes'

'Bunches of Grapes'
'Night Swans'
'Reverie'.
>   Yours faithfully
>   Edward Thomas.

2

Thomas softens the possible effect of his 14 August 1902 unfavourable Daily Chronicle *review of de la Mare's* Songs of Childhood *by referring to his more positive 17 May 1904* Daily Chronicle *review of the adult novel* Henry Brocken.

>   THE WEALD,
>   Nr. SEVENOAKS.
>   18 August 1906

Dear Sir,

I thank you heartily for your compliment & your kind leave to use poems from the 'Songs of Childhood' in my anthology. I wish I could insert half the book. 'Henry Brocken' was a great joy to me. I only know these two & I should be grateful if you would let me know of any others out or to come.

>   Yours very truly
>   Edward Thomas

3

On the day of this letter, Thomas tells Bottomley he has selected de la Mare's 'Child in the story awakes' *and* 'Bunches of Grapes' *for* The Pocket Book. 'Reverie' (beginning 'When slim Sophia') is lovely". *Thomas is reviewing books for the* Daily Chronicle *at least once a week at this time.*

>   THE WEALD,
>   Nr. SEVENOAKS.
>   27 August 1906

Dear Sir,

I am very glad to hear you are publishing some more poetry. If you care to let me know a few days before reviewers' topics are sent out, I shall ask for it, & have no doubt I can do you whatever service praise may be – But I have never dreamed of collecting my reviews. I live by them & that seems to me to be wonderful enough without sending the poor things out in fine raiment to beg once more. For as I dislike writing about books and do it in haste & in such abundance, I assume it is valueless – It is good of you to ask about my books. I began at an early age in 1897 – since then I have published:

'Horae Solitariae'	Duckworth	2/6.
'Oxford'	Black	20/-
'Rose Acre papers'	Brown Langham	1/6
'Beautiful Wales'	Black	20/-
'The Heart of England'	Dent	20/- just coming.

But the expensive books were written to order and the little books of essays are very early.

Believe me

Yours very truly

Edward Thomas.

4

Thomas and his family move from Kent to Hampshire. The "new book" is de la Mare's Poems. *Thomas echoes the criticism of de la Mare's archaic language in his largely positive 9 November 1906* Daily Chronicle *review of* Poems.

BERRYFIELD COTTAGE,
ASHFORD,
PETERSFIELD
31 October 1906

My dear Sir,

May I use one of the poems from your new book in my anthology if at the last moment I can make room? I thought of 'Keep Innocency'. I like the book enormously and one or two pages will be good enough to let me say so, though I had not the space I could have wished. I only grumble at your 'ev'n' instead of 'even' & so on, especially as it did not seem to be needed by the rhythm.

The above address is, I hope, a permanent one.
   Yours sincerely
      Edward Thomas.

5

De la Mare lives in Anerley. All three de la Mare poems appear in The Pocket
Book, *not, Thomas writes to Bottomley on 27 August 1906, "because they are
the best, but on the whole the fittest."*

BERRYFIELD COTTAGE,
ASHFORD,
PETERSFIELD
14 November 1906

Dear Mr de la Mare,

   I was very glad to have your letter this morning. You are the only
man I do not know who has ever written to me about my reviews
& knowing your work I cannot but be happy. And yet I feel that
even I could do so much better – if only I had time. My article was
only a hasty review: I had not time to order or make clear the
thoughts & emotions your 'Poems' suggest. But to have pleased
you is everything & to talk like this is my vanity. So thank you
again & may I look forward to seeing you in London. May I call?
When I am in London I often happen to be in Anerley (which I
shall like a little better now).

   I am using 'Keep Innocency' & (probably) 'Bunches of Grapes'
& 'The Child in the Story awakens' also in my Anthology. I will
mention the publishers.

   About 'Ev'n' I think you can count on your readers making it a
grave monosyllable without printing it so.

   My other review of you – a very scrappy little one – will appear
in the Bookman.

      Yours sincerely
         Edward Thomas.

6

BERRYFIELD COTTAGE,
ASHFORD,
PETERSFIELD
9 January 1907

Dear Mr. de la Mare,

Thank you for saying that I may come some day, & I shall be happy to when I am next in Anerley which will very likely be at the end of this month; but I will let you know exactly when & hope that you will be free. I am sorry you have had illness in the house. I can easily guess what that means in narrow quarters, in Anerley, in winter, with four children in the house. I hope you are all well again.

Yours sincerely
Edward Thomas.

7

In a letter to Bottomley written on the same day, Thomas records his decision to quote de la Mare's sonnet, 'The Happy Encounter', in his introduction to The Book of the Open Air, *and his relief when he realises "that in reviewing de la Mare's 1st book years ago I quoted all of 'Lovelocks'. Thank God."*

BERRYFIELD COTTAGE,
ASHFORD,
PETERSFIELD
7 March 1907

Dear Mr. de la Mare,

Will you come and stay with us for Easter – from the Thursday before Good Friday until the Tuesday after or for whatever modification of that providence allows you? We invite your wife, too, but ask you particularly so that we shall have two chances of catching you instead of one. My visits to town have been so hurried & crammed that I could only have got to you for certain fixed hours, a thing I abhor, so I have put off our meeting for too long. But perhaps I can catch you in town next Tuesday or Wednesday for tea or dinner? I am not yet sure which day is free. Let me know as soon as you can.

Yours sincerely
Edward Thomas.

8

In this letter, the "interval" is graphically represented in Thomas's handwriting by a series of gaps between the words describing the discomfort of the railway journey.

> BERRYFIELD COTTAGE,
> ASHFORD,
> PETERSFIELD
> 10 March 1907

Dear Mr. de la Mare,

I am sorry your wife can't come. But I gather that you can come for a day. Do, & if possible stay one night, since a day with a long uncomfortable railway journey at each end is nothing at all but an interval.

Tuesday suits me best. I have been trying to think of a place where we could meet in the City but I know it so badly that I can only suggest George Yard in Lombard Street – just inside on the left is a 'Mecca' (I think) & I will meet you at the top of the steps which lead down to it. I believe there are 2 George Yards but this one contains the Deutsche Bank & is nearly opposite the Crédit Lyonnais. I hope that is clear: the time Tuesday next between 5.30 & 5.40.

> Yours sincerely
> Edward Thomas.

9

The deleted "Mr" in Thomas's salutation to de la Mare marks a moment of awareness of this deepening friendship.
Horae Solitariae *is Thomas's 1902 collection of short sketches and essays.*
In his very positive March 1907 Bookman *review of* The Heart of England, *Arthur Ransome calls it "a beautiful disturbing thing". The same issue has a full-length feature on Thomas, celebrating him as critic and "country essayist", also written by Ransome.*
Roger Ingpen, de la Mare's brother-in-law, worked as a publisher's reader for Hutchinson at this time. He becomes an important contact for Thomas, publishing his collection of poems in 1917.

> Devizes

Dear ~~Mr~~ de la Mare,

Of course I don't mind & am simply grateful. I shall arrange to see Mr Ingpen — is he Roger Ingpen? — when I am up on or about April 7. I shall send you my Horae as soon as I can. Tell me what, if anything, occurs to you on reading what is best in my 'Heart of England.' — I am no good for a little now. I have just had 4 days in & about Chepstow & am now walking about the Downs & Savernake Forest in Wiltshire. We must meet soon & I do hope you will come on Good Friday – I mean the night before — & I suppose you will as you do not mention it — Thursday's 5 o'clock train until Saturday's 10.20 at least.

Yours ever

Edward Thomas.

10

The "My" that now appends Thomas's salutation marks the two men's developing intimacy. Ingpen had introduced de la Mare to Lobban, editor of the Bookman., *for whom de la Mare had been reviewing for Lobban since November 1905.*

BERRYFIELD COTTAGE,
ASHFORD,
PETERSFIELD
21 March 1907

My dear de la Mare,

Here is my Horae mainly the product of Oxford nights in 1899 & 1900 & of kippers and tea in Earlsfield & Balham in 1901: as such, forgive what they lack, but what they are please say what you like about.

I saw Ingpen today for a little while & liked him: we are to meet early in April.

My 'Pocket Book of Poems & Songs for the Open Air' comes out in April, I expect. Perhaps you would like to do it for Lobban.

Yours

Edward Thomas

11

*In a 4 September 1906 letter to Bottomley, Thomas calls the 'Earth Children',
from* The Heart of England, *"the best thing of all".*

De la Mare wrote a story called 'The Earth Child' in his self-made magazine
The Horn Book *in 1897. Thomas reports in a 22 April 1907 letter to
Bottomley that de la Mare prefers Thomas's reviews to his writing about
landscapes and people, "which annoys me."*
Bottomley's 1945 Welsh Review *article recollects that both he and de la Mare
suggested sections of* The Heart of England *might have better effect if
conceived from the first as poetry. The note for letter 17 quotes from this article.
Thomas was discussing with Ingpen the possibility of writing a life and criticism of Richard Jefferies for Hutchinson, eventually published by them in 1909
to much acclaim.*

BERRYFIELD COTTAGE,
ASHFORD,
PETERSFIELD
23 March 1907

Dear de la Mare,

We are very sorry you can't come. I think I quite understand. &
I know I should be uneasy in your case. So come as soon as you
can and we will meet in town on Monday the 8th at 5.30 as before
unless you know a better place. I am eager to hear what you will
say of the two books, & glad you liked the Earth Children — I was
afraid they looked rather a townsman's make-up but when you say
they have an earthiness about them I am delighted (though not
quite convinced.) By this time you will have had Horae & my letter
mentioning that I saw Ingpen on my way through town last
Thursday.

Until Monday fortnight then. Our kindest regards & good
wishes for your wife & the sick children.

Yours ever
Edward Thomas

12

Henry Nevinson, an influential journalist on the staff of the Daily Chronicle,
where most of Thomas's reviews were published, also worked for the Nation
and the Manchester Guardian.

4 April 1907

My dear de la Mare,

Nevinson has just asked me to produce a poet who would send

him a batch of lyrics to select from for 'The Nation'. Will you send
him some? or send them to me first? None should exceed 20 lines,
I think. They pay well, I believe, and it would be a useful connection, for they want a poem every week.

I was sorry to run away in such a hurry on Tuesday.

Yours ever

Edward Thomas

—   P.T.O.

Nevinson's address —
    H W Nevinson
    c/o The Nation
      14 Henrietta St.,
        Covent Garden, W.C..

13

*Together with de la Mare, W.H. Davies was the contemporary poet Thomas
rated most highly at this time, writing to Bottomley on 24 January 1906 that
"I think he has immortal moments". Thomas provided Davies with much
financial and literary support, sharing his small study cottage with him for
most of 1906. In the April 1907* Bookman *he described Davies's* The Soul's
Destroyer *as "some of the most beautiful and poignant poetry of our day".*
Nevinson covered the 1905-1907 Russian Revolution for the Manchester
Guardian.
'Alone' appears in de la Mare's The Listeners *in 1912.*

BERRYFIELD COTTAGE,
ASHFORD,
PETERSFIELD
11 April 1907

My dear de la Mare

I have waited in the hope of hearing from Nevinson. for I sent
him your M.S. straightway. But as I gave him your address he may
have written to you. Or it is possible he may have hurried away to
Russia. I liked the poems, but especially 'Alone' & I sent them all
to him as I did not want to interfere with his judgement which is
as a rule very good though a little oldfashioned perhaps.

Keep the 'Heart of England' as long as you like.

I may be in town next week to introduce William Davies to a cabinet minister and another member of Parliament in the hope of getting him a little on the Civil list.

> Yours ever
> Edward Thomas

14

Thomas includes Davies's 'Autumn', 'A Drinking Song' and lines from the title poem, 'The Soul's Destroyer' in The Pocket Book.

> BERRYFIELD COTTAGE,
> ASHFORD,
> PETERSFIELD.
> 16 April 1907

My dear de la Mare,

I am glad to hear that Nevinson liked your work. May they go on sending you proofs.

Shall we meet at the 'Mecca' at 5.40 on Friday? Unless you write against it, I will be there.

John Burns is the minister – I knew you would find the good things in 'The Soul's Destroyer' All of 'Love Absent' is good & the drinking song & Autumn & Beauty's Light. He will go on. He has been writing hard all the winter & is consequently a little dejected now in the Spring. Perhaps I will bring him along on Friday.

> In haste but
> Ever yours
> Edward Thomas

15

> BERRYFIELD COTTAGE,
> ASHFORD,
> PETERSFIELD.
> 2 May 1907
> [postmarked MY 3 07]

Can you meet me at 6 on Monday next outside the tea shop at the corner of Bouverie Street, Strand?   E.T.

16

> BERRYFIELD COTTAGE,
> ASHFORD,
> PETERSFIELD.
> Monday
> [postmarked JU 3 07]

Do meet me outside the tea shop at corner of Bouverie Street, Fleet Street, at 10 to 6 tomorrow, Tuesday.

ET..

17

Some of the content of Thomas's meetings with de la Mare at this time surfaces in Bottomley's recollections in the 1945 Welsh Review, *in which Bottomley recalls suggesting to Thomas that paragraphs in* The Heart of England *"would make their effect better if they had been conceived in actual verse from the first. He replied 'It is strange you should say this. I spent the night at de la Mare's on my way North to you, and he said almost the same thing.' [...] I urged the experiment on him. He smiled and only said 'I do not know how.'"*

c/o Gordon Bottomley Esq,
  Well Knowe,
    Cartmel,
      by Carnforth.

BERRYFIELD COTTAGE,
ASHFORD,
PETERSFIELD.
[in pencil, ca 19 June 07]

Can I spend next Thursday evening with you, meeting you in town somewhere at about 5.30. Suggest time & place.   ET..

18

Berryfield Cottage
 18 June 1907

46, FITZROY STREET,
FITZROY SQUARE,
W.

My dear de la Mare,

 I haven't heard from you yet & am hoping this will reach you in time to let you know I have had to change my plans & get home tomorrow afternoon. Perhaps you were unable to meet me tomorrow in any case. But forgive me, if I disappoint you, & we can soon meet again. Can you come down do you think? I mean this as an open invitation.

    Yours ever

      Edward Thomas

19

Thomas travelled to research his prose books, writing copious notes and asking literary friends for suggestions of written material.

In June de la Mare's family moved from a cramped flat to a house, still in Anerley. In August they went on holiday in Ockley, Surrey. De la Mare worked in London in the week and joined them at weekends.

Thomas was discussing a book on Borrow with Methuen. He did some research for it in 1907 and 8 but the project was delayed and then fell through. He eventually wrote the book for Chapman and Hall. It was published in 1912. The "uninteresting" Chronicle *reviews includes Bottomley's* Chambers of Imagery *on 5 August, which is "not always wrought up to the condition of poetry." De la Mare however, as Thomas reports to Bottomley in early June of one* Chambers of Imagery *poem, had a different opinion: "Oh, de la Mare likes your 'Dairymaids to Pan'."*

The rhyme of "ever" and "weather" in the last line, emphasized by Thomas's use of spacing, is likely to be a tribute to de la Mare's verse.

                BERRYFIELD COTTAGE,
                ASHFORD,
                PETERSFIELD
                10 August 1907

My dear de la Mare,

    We are sorry you are not free. I go to Jefferies country (c/o Miss Smith, Broome Farm, nr Swindon, Wiltshire) on Tuesday & leave there about the 30th. I should very much like to come & see you at your Elizabethan house on the 31st or Sept. 1st , but doubt if I shall have time. Then I don't know where Ockley is. — I am very busy, choked with proofs, correspondence, endless books to read. The Jefferies is in an early state of chaos as yet, & I am to see Mrs Jefferies again in a day or two, C.J. Longman later. The Chronicle has printed 3 or 4 things of mine in the past week or so, several of them signed, but all uninteresting: before that they forswore me for weeks — I can forswear nobody who will give me money. Well if I can't see you at Ockley or in town about the 31st. I shall see you in town in the middle of September. I hope you can write a little. As for me, I have filled 4 notebooks since The Heart of England & used not a line of them. I have a secret (how long it will remain one I don't know), & please keep it one — I am to write a book on Borrow to appear 6 months after the Jefferies probably! If you know of anything on him in magazines or books — the same of Jefferies — do let me know names & dates, as I am a slow, muddled & ill-informed writer.

Yours ever with wishes for good weather
Edward Thomas

20

19 Cambria Place,
New Swindon,
Wiltshire
28 August 1907.
[postmarked AU 29 07, redirected twice,
with final postmark AU 31 07, Capel]

Can we meet at the corner of Bouverie Street next Tuesday (Sept. 3) at 5.45
Edward Thomas

21

Capel was very near Ockley, Surrey, where the de la Mare family were on holiday. Thomas's fascination with de la Mare's address reflects his perennial interest in place names.

Thomas's meticulous research methods are evident in the topographical and genealogical bias of the first Jefferies chapters. The first chapter traces the landscape that drew on imaginatively all his life and was heralded by the publisher's reader Edward Garnett as the best piece of criticism on Jefferies ever.

19 Cambria Place,
New Swindon,
Wiltshire
31 August 1907

Dear de la Mare,

Your letter has only just reached me & it is 9.15 p.m. So as you are only certainly at Capel until the 2nd I can hardly come. I am very sorry. But perhaps you will be able to meet me at the corner of Bouverie Street on Tuesday at 5.45? I wrote to you suggesting that on Thursday. Your address is fascinating. Mine is not, if you know New Swindon. But I have been all day on the Downs Except when I have been at Parish Registers & in public houses. I have made no great discoveries, but have got many pleasing trifles about Jefferies & his family & of course no end of notes about the country. I am not dissatisfied. But I am anxious to be back at my reviewing. For I haven't written a line since I came here nearly 3 weeks ago, & so have earned no money.

There is a good deal to detest in Borrow & I expect we agree about him, tho I knew him pretty well. He is a superb brute who lived if ever a man did (at least on paper), a kind of coarse, large, <u>active</u> Charles Lamb.

Well, I will look for you on Tuesday.

Ever yours
Edward Thomas

22

Thomas is working at the British Museum to prepare for his field research on Jefferies.

BERRYFIELD COTTAGE,
ASHFORD,
PETERSFIELD.
2 November 1907

My dear de la Mare,

I am coming to town for a fortnight on Monday (the 4th) to work at the Museum. We can meet, I hope. The Museum would not be a very out of the way place for you, would it ? Could you meet me at the entrance gate on Wednesday at 5.50 ? If not suggest

another day. In very great haste
     Yours ever (& with salutations to your wife)
     Edward Thomas

23

De la Mare was asked to write the 11 September 1907 Guardian *obituary of the poet and novelist Mary Coleridge. Since her 1902 review of his* Songs of Childhood *in the* Monthly Review *she had met with him regularly to discuss his poetry. The obituary results in an introduction to the influential writer Edith Sichel.*

Thomas's congratulations on de la Mare's success in reviewing Herbert Trench's 1907 New Poems *are heartfelt. In a 26 December 1907 letter to Bottomley, Thomas refers to Trench's 1901* Deirdre Wed *as "most beautiful [...]. Yet I know I like it because with great good luck I might have done it myself." He also quotes this passage in the 11 June 1908* Morning Post *review of Trench, calling it "one of the most beautiful similes we know."*

De la Mare's December Bookman *review seems to agree with this letter. He refers to Trench's* New Poems *as "fine, original, vivid work", but includes the proviso that one or two poems "suffer from over-emphasis, and are a little burdened by the author's unusual gift of language. This occurs only, perhaps, when the emotional impetus is not quite so personal."*

Thomas's criticism of Trench's poems indicates his value of spontaneity, highly prized by him in W.H. Davies's work.

The reference to cheap Sunday trains reflects Thomas's awareness of de la Mare's financial situation, underpaid in his work at Anglo American Oil. In a 11 October 1907 letter to Bottomley, he describes de la Mare as "almost poor".

De la Mare's 'Characters from Shakespeare' were published in Poems *in 1906 which Thomas reviewed very favourably in the 9 November* Daily Chronicle *and the December 1910* English Review, *where he praises the 'Characters from Shakespeare' for having "an all but independent life" from their subject-matter. In 1914, he selects 'Ophelia' from this collection for his* Flowers I Love *anthology, published in 1916.*

              BERRYFIELD COTTAGE,
              ASHFORD,
              PETERSFIELD.
              19 November 1907

My dear de la Mare,
    I am sorry I could not manage to see you again. I left on Friday & I had very few moments to spare. But I am not going away till

after Christmas & shall see you in town about December 4 I hope. I don't know if there are any cheap Sunday trains nowadays. I wish you could come down. You were lucky to get Trench. He is good: some of his Deirdre Wed is beautiful. He knows your work by the way & likes it but disapproves of Shakespearean Characters. I met him for a brief lunch last week: he had sent me his book — but I have had no chance to review it. The new book I have hardly looked at. I liked the first poem but remember thinking it a bit made up & it was unfortunate that it resembled the finest poem in the world.

I hope you are all well again,

Yours ever

Edward Thomas.

24

Ingpen had recently introduced de la Mare to the poet John Freeman. Living close to each other, both working in the city and writing poetry late into the evenings, they quickly become friends and mutual supporters of each other's verse. De la Mare reviews Freeman's Twenty Poems *in the April 1909* Bookman *and, like Thomas, highlights both 'Prayer to My Lord' which he calls 'most beautiful' and 'Happy Death'. Freeman later becomes a good friend of Thomas as well. Thomas's comments reveal his keen appreciation of precise writing. Later, in 1914, he starts writing directly to Freeman, expressing disillusionment with Freeman's writing and again emphasising the need for precision. Thomas is about to go to Minsmere to write* Jefferies.

THE WEALD,

Nr SEVENOAKS

Ashford

16 December 1907

My dear de la Mare,

I liked reading the poems you sent me. The first poem – the one out of, 'The Puppet Master' – showed at once that he could write & had a special individual feeling for words. Then 'Prayer to My Lord' seemed to me very fine; 'Waterpools' also & in the main 'After flight'; 'The Men who loved the cause that never died'; & everything of 'Happy Death' except the title. But I find I am going through them all except the last long one — 'The Plighted Queen'

& that had an untransmuted allegorical feeling that disagreed with me. Often the writing is admirable – I mean that I feel in reading, quite suddenly & with a thrill, that here are words arranged in a foreordained manner which I can't explain. You must be annoyed at my only making these very vague & general remarks, for I am terribly busy trying to get rid of a lot of trivial work before I leave home. That will be on the 27th of this month most likely. If so, can we meet for tea? I will let you know positively as soon as I can. I have just filled a small box with roots and am sending them to you by rail, carriage paid. They aren't as much as I meant, but the Michaelmas daisies & other big things are so clotted with moist earth that they would weigh too much. I will send some more in the Spring perhaps. The feathery stuff here & there is a kind of Saxifrage, green all the year round with a beautiful ivory flower, & it spreads rapidly. Plant it in loose earth so that it is covered up all but the green tops & it will soon be right. In the bit of newspaper — & I hope not crushed – are some big African poppy roots. At the bottom is one piece of Michaelmas daisy and one piece of a big knapweed. Then there are several pieces of pink, I think some Canterbury bell, some forget me not, & at the top several roots of Japanese anemone which I don't feel very certain about, & in any case they will be diffident at first. Also there are 4 roots of holly-hock. In the Spring there ought to be many seedlings I could send. Here is a packet of Columbine seeds from my garden at The Weald.

> With good wishes to you all
> Ever yours
> Edward Thomas

P.S. I now find the box won't go till Wednesday which is a nuisance, but it ought to be all right.

25

Thomas takes a cottage in Minsmere to write Jefferies. *The "piecemeal" approach reflects his interest in the particular, later so evident in his poems. He accompanies the vivid description of Minsmere with a drawing of a church. The reference to tumbling bones shows his awareness of de la Mare's fascination with death and the macabre, as in the very first of de la Mare's published stories, 'Kismet', in the 1895* Sketch, *in which a returning seaman finds himself coming home in a carrier that bears his wife's coffin.*

Minsmere
nr Dunwich
Saxmundham
12 February 1908

My dear de la Mare,

This is only a word to say that I am not forgetful out here, but quite unable to write a letter worth writing. For six weeks I have been writing on Jefferies every day but one or two I had to steal for reviewing, & writing so hard that I am almost at an end of my first draft. So I expect soon to leave here & if possible to see you on my way through town. I can't say anything about Jefferies except that I fear I have been swamped by the necessity, in the case of a writer as yet almost uncriticized, of taking him piece meal, rather than of making the sweeping whole I should have liked better. My work will probably be good chiefly as an anthology with fingerposts which is a sad thing to have spent nearly a year over. However, it may turn out more than that, & in the distress of getting to an end I can't take a cheerful view. I have gone far beyond Hutchinson's minimum & I want Ingpen to tell me whether they mind 100,000 or even 120,000 instead of 80,000? — I forget if you know this coast? This little coastguard station of black cottages stands far from all other houses on the edge of a sandy cliff which is the end of a fine undulating moor of gorse heather & moss. There are two miles of the cliff & on either side the seaboard is perfectly flat dyked country onto which we look down & see windmills & black cattle, with very gentle humps of ploughland & then pines more inland: but hills nowhere. We are at one end of the cliff; at the other is Dunwich old church, a pale ruin, a tower and a roofless nave, the last window of which is at the very edge of the cliff & the East End & the graveyard drop out their skeletons daily on to the beach, so that the children handle skulls & thighbones as carelessly as apples. Inland is chiefly a flat corn country, most dreary at this season, & as I say, not a hill to be seen. You have to walk a mile to hear a thrush sing. So I am a little tired of it. The only things I don't tire of are the pebbles on the beach of an infinite variety of shapes & colours. I pick them up by the score & take them home. Their shapes are so fascinating – some faint original predisposition, I suppose, has arranged that they shall roll over & over & take the pear or the bean or the disc shape & no other, which is sometimes a cheerful thought & sometimes not.

How are you all? My boy has been through measles. I have been on the whole very well, what with the east wind, solitude & medicine, but work has brought me back nearly to my original state of desperate listlessness.

Please write & say something. Remember me to your wife & the children & to Ingpen.

> Ever yours
> Edward Thomas.

26

De la Mare took regular holidays with Elfie in Southwold before they were married.

Thomas continues to show a fascination with place and personal names, an interest de la Mare was to replicate later in the year in the names he uses in The Three Mulla-Mulgars. *De la Mare names the skull Thomas sends him Moses. He keeps it reverentially in an unopened decorated box all his life, berating Laurence and Theresa Whistler for a lack of proper respect when they open the box in 1955.*

The mutual support enjoyed by Thomas and de la Mare is evident in de la Mare's offer to look at the Jefferies *manuscript and Thomas's reference to de la Mare's long hours working in the City – de la Mare's workload had just been doubled without a rise in pay, writing becoming impossible for him.*

The neighbour's child is seventeen year old Hope Webb, formally a protégé of Thomas's wife's when she worked as a governess. The second coeval is Thomas's schoolfriend Arthur Hardy.

> Minsmere
> nr Dunwich
> Suffolk
> 19 February 1908

My dear de la Mare,

Thank you for your letter. How stupid of me to forget you knew this coast, for you did tell me. I have only been to Southwold once, but there is no purpose in walking in a flat country & the walk wearied me. I did like the gorse & the common with Southwold above it, also the name of BOGGIS over one shop. Would you really like a skull? Of course as they roll down the cliff they divide — the lower jaw, chin & c coming apart from the nose & the dome.

But if I can get a whole I will. Only, now they have fenced in the base of the cliff to keep out the sea & the disinterments will be fewer for a time. Some are reburied, but there is no great care, & as to thighbones, their rich red-golden brown is always to be seen. You probably know that the skulls get very brittle & cocoanut coloured, so you will have to be careful. I wonder what you will make of it. Will you really see Helen's eyes? It would be easier for me to see the skull while the girl talked to me, I am afraid. I don't believe I really have any imagination, certainly not enough to distinguish between it & reality. But I feel sure it is beyond what is called reality, that it is something fit for & even aware of infinite & eternal things. Jefferies & Maeterlinck believe that it is so weak — they call it the soul – simply because we do not as yet admit its existence & have never tried to nourish it & let it have its way. I think it may be found to be life itself to which flesh mind & c are only aids, that it is what enables us to feel & know the divine in all things, is itself the divine to wh [sic] the rest of the universe responds according as we have or have not cut off our communi-cation by pampering flesh & mind: [which is not very clear & maybe pure metaphor, I mean bad, metaphor.] So that only by imagination can we see things flesh & spirit as they are, only by it understand the life of things & take images of them about with us for ever. That is the only hypothesis to suit my own experience. You ought to read Jefferies' 'Story of My Heart'. Will you if I lend it to you? I have had nobody at all to discuss it with so that I have come only to my customary rhetorical & general conclusions about it. When you have read it you will not think of water & wine in the relations you suggest.

I am so glad you have got Energy even if congested. My case is just the opposite, lack of Energy expanded. And so the Jefferies is getting to an end —. I wish you would write more now; & yet when I think of it it is wonderful you write at all after your long days every day in Town. — I would gladly lend you parts of my 'Jefferies' but you have no idea what my MSS are like – something like a lawn intersected with mole runs & dotted with mole heaps & worm casts. I continually add in the margin, on top & between lines: I only indicate the pages of my innumerable quotations & I alter the order of the paragraphs & c very often. It will be quite hard work for me to follow all the signposts. But when it is copied & typed you shall see it & help to amend it.

My health began by improving rapidly, but then I began to get very fond of one of the children of my neighbours (they are retired Anglo Indians, friends of friends of mine), & she left a month ago to go to school & the place has become chiefly superficies ever since. She is 17, a particularly lovely age to me because when I was that age I knew only two of my coevals, one I married & the other is in South America, & in the presence of this new one I had the sharpest pains & pleasures of retrospection, longing & …. I am now making absurd attempts to return to that period by means of letters! You see I have a young head on my decrepit shoulders.

I expect to leave here on March 2 or 3 & though I can't get to Anerley I hope we can meet in town. Also I have thoughts of coming up to town by a cheap train next Tuesday, the 25th, and should like to meet you then. Could you be at the corner of Bouverie St at 5.45 on the 25th? I will let you know for certain if I am coming, either on that day or before & unless I have heard against it will assume you can be there.

> With best wishes to you all,
> Ever yours
> Edward Thomas

27

"Philoprogenitiveness": love of children denoted by the formation of the back of the head, a term from phrenology.

> Ashford
> Petersfield
> 13 March 1908

My dear de la Mare,

I very much wanted to write a long letter to you when I had got yours — never mind your today — but in truth I was not to be trusted with a pen; it would have been but a vain & unhappy attempt to fling myself on to paper, partly to answer to your letter, partly to get rid of a hundred things knowing my mind which has been in Hell these many days. In short I am not better but worse & find living — I write now calmly enough — only just possible. I should not say these cryptic things I know, but tho you cannot divine you will not be angry & it is a moment's relief to me. —

Well, I am to be in town on Tuesday next. Can we meet at Bouverie Street at 5.50? I can't go home with you but can spare the time until 7.30 or so I hope you will be free. If not, write at once & say if Wednesday is good for you. I shall have less time, but can probably be free until near 7.

I can't answer your letter as I have a crowd of utterly uncongenial books to read & review, but about the skull. I think the jawbone has been some time in the sea, but the cavity certainly has not; so whether they are related or met by chance in the sand I cannot swear. As to the bump, are you sure that the skull's is that called of philoprogenitiveness? I don't know if it is more than a superstition which schoolboys adopt. But I believe I have the one so named myself.

> Yours ever
> Edward Thomas

28

Thomas and de la Mare's children frequently stay at each other's houses for long or shorter visits.
The weather had a strong effect on Thomas's moods and writing.

> Ashford
> Petersfield
> 9 April 1908

Dear de la Mare,

Can you come down for Easter or any part of Easter? We haven't a lot of room but if you could bring one of the children that could easily be managed & we should like it. Let me know what you think.

I am now physically stronger, but as soon as my thoughts stray back to myself the same East Wind blows. On the other hand the hour of sunset on Tuesday when I was walking back from Selborne through a steep valley with oaks & an invisible but noisy stream & no one about & the wind quite gone — that kept me quite unconscious and entranced.

> Yours ever
> Edward Thomas

I am in the midst of a lot of poor books very dull & hard to tackle & quite out of my line, or I would write a letter.

29

Written in pencil, a souvenir post card captioned 'Fishing Boats in Mounts Bay, Penzance'.

[postmarked 29 June 1908, Penzance and redirected JU 30 08, Anerley]

Marazione
Will meet you tomorrow ★ at 5.50 as usual
E.T.

★ Tuesday

30

The passage probably refers to Jefferies's death-bed return to Christianity, included in the penultimate chapter in Jefferies.

Thomas's growing estimation of de la Mare as a critic is indicated in his request that de la Mare look at this passage and in their discussion of it in subsequent letters. This coincides with recognition of de la Mare's reviews from a number of quarters. The retiring Bookman *editor, Lobban, states that his reviews have helped set the paper on a better footing; Newbolt is very impressed with his May review of Herrick, and in June Edith Sichel invites him to attend her literary salon, introducing him to Bruce Richmond, editor of the* Times Literary Supplement, *who had given* Henry Brocken *a favourable review and who subsequently offers de la Mare work on the paper.*

[July 1908?]

Dear de la Mare,

Here is the disputable passage, beginning half way down the front page. If you could read it & make any suggestions & return it to me not later than next Monday I should be grateful. In a great hurry

Yours ever
Edward Thomas.

31

Thomas continues the discussion begun in the previous letter. His opinion of his Jefferies *is low, as is usually the case when he is in the process of writing prose books. His reference to his own writing as 'hopelessly mixed' reflects his description in the book of Jefferies's essays as 'irregular, patchwork'.*

Friday
24 July 1908

My dear de la Mare,

Thanks. You are mostly right I think & I dislike the subject but cannot – in a commonplace biography — avoid it. Hence my contemptuous attitude perhaps. The conversion means nothing to me: his life & his best work is everything, his death an accident. And if a set of people who care nothing for his work are to make a fuss about the last scene I am going to allow myself the pleasure of showing my opinion of them.

Believe me I would willingly show you more of the book. But as a rule criticism & c is hopelessly mixed with crude fact & long quotations. It really is a rotten book. So I can only send you the final chapter. I know it to be horribly vague & insufficient — but it really is recapitulation & all the real criticism is in the body of the book. Please let me have it back quickly & if you can say anything don't be afraid please. Remember me to your wife & the children – we still hope to see you here someday, but it rests with you to suggest a day.

Yours ever
Edward Thomas

32

BERRYFIELD COTTAGE,
ASHFORD,
PETERSFIELD.
26 July 1908.
[postmarked JY 27 08]

Can you be at the corner of Bouverie Street on Tuesday at 5.50?
E.T..

33

The manuscript is Jefferies.

> BERRYFIELD COTTAGE,
> ASHFORD,
> PETERSFIELD.
> Wednesday
> [postmarked JY 29 08]

Sorry you could not come. Can you return the M.S. tonight? I want to send off the whole to Hutchinson on Thursday. Please make any comments that occur to you unless of course they are purely destructive – as they well might be.   ET..

34

Sir Edward Grey, Foreign Secretary and lover of literature, was a prime mover behind de la Mare's July 1908 award of £200 to set him free to do literary work. The money lasted till the summer of 1910. This enabled him to take up writing fulltime.
Thomas dedicated Jefferies *to the writer and naturalist W.H. Hudson.*

                                                Ashford
My dear de la Mare,
    Thanks for the MS.& your letter. I made use of your suggestions as a rule, e.g. putting in a few words about J's unpopularity at school & suggesting that it was the result of that something repellent in him which you (and Sir Edward Grey to Hudson) see in his writing at times. It can't be defined except by comparing it with a trick of voice or manner that offends. Of course he is emphatic & he is capable of a certain viciousness which one dislikes particularly in a man so pathetically unworldly & alone. A snarl, perhaps you haven't noticed it. Nobody has a really kindly thing to say of him personally. But it may have been simply the awkwardness of an unsocial animal.
    You ask me to define Nature. I used it vulgarly for all that is not man, perhaps because man contemplates it so, as outside himself, & has a sort of belief that Nature is only a house, furniture & c round about him. It is not my belief, & I don't opposed [sic]

Nature to Man. Quite the contrary Man seems to me a very little part of Nature & the part I enjoy least. But civilisation has estranged us superficially from Nature, & towns make it possible for a man to live as if a millionaire could really produce all the necessities of life, food, drink, clothes, vehicles & c, then a tombstone. I believe some do live so. But I can't write about this being specially busy after walking to Goodwood races & back yesterday & getting overtired & behind with my work.

> Yours ever
> Edward Thomas

35

> Ashford
> nr Petersfield
> [in pencil, 19 July - 9 August 1908?]

My dear de la Mare,

I hope you are better now. But if not please return these proofs & don't bother. In any case I should like them back by Friday. With our love to you all

> Ever yours
> Edward Thomas.

I am finishing the Jefferies introduction & too too busy.

36

This undated pencilled note is placed at the end of the Bodleian album. The references to October, to a cottage, to a repeated visit to Anerley, the relatively formal tone of the letter, and examination of other letters to de la Mare suggest the year is likely to be 1908, although 1909 is a possibility.

> 21, BEDFORD STREET,
> LONDON, W.C.

My dear de la Mare,

My wife has just gone to Anerley for the afternoon but will you excuse me yet again if I don't come? I feel sure I shall relieve you thus as well as disappoint you.

I shall be up again about October 8. But did I tell you there is a spare room close to us which you can have supposing we can't make room in the cottage?

    Yours ever
        Edward Thomas

37

The 'Royal Commission on Ancient Monuments in Wales and Monmouthshire' that heads this paper is where Thomas was working, unhappily, mainly in London, as Assistant Secretary from August to December 1908.

De la Mare hands in notice to Anglo-American Oil on 15 September 1908, deciding to live by writing and his recently acquired Civil List pension. He is now writing regular unsigned reviews for the Times Literary Supplement, *his first review, of George Russell's* Some 3d. bits, *appearing in mid September 1908, his second, of* The Potters of Tadcaster, *a fortnight later. In 1909 the* Times Literary Supplement *publishes his first front-page article, which is on Poe.*

Thomas's wish for de la Mare to write "something you entirely like and something long" is soon fulfilled when de la Mare starts work on The Three Mulla-Mulgars *and* The Return.

Grant Richards worked for Jonathan Cape. He published Thomas's The Pocket Book. *In October 1908 Thomas proposed to him the possibility of a book on Nature in English Literature or Nature in English Poetry.*

ROYAL COMMISSION ON ANCIENT MONUMENTS
IN WALES AND MONMOUTHSHIRE
                        Rusham Road
                        Balham, S.W..
                        9 October 1908

My dear de la Mare,

Will Thursday next suit you? I should arrive about 6.45 I expect. What is my best station? If not Thursday let it be Tuesday or Wednesday. I have read your reviews in the 'Times.' Of course they did not give you a full chance, but they were excellent. I am eager to see you doing something you entirely like & something long, too. May I speak about you to Grant Richards?

    Yours ever
        Edward Thomas

38

With the freedom from his drudgery at Anglo-American Oil, de la Mare throws himself into writing, setting himself to complete 2000 words a day of the story referred to here – The Three Mulla-Mulgars, *which originated in a series of tales told to his children on Sunday afternoons. Many of the unusual character names are lifted from* Purchas His Pilgrimes *by Samuel Purchas, the seventeenth-century travel writer.*

Thomas plans to leave his post at the Royal Commission, which he hates.

De la Mare is negotiating writing a biography for Hutchinson, where Ingpen now works, and is casting about for a subject. Thomas cautions de la Mare against choosing the Gothic novelist, William Beckford, writer of Vathek. *De la Mare in the event drops the idea and never attempts a biography.*

~~BERRYFIELD,~~
13 Rusham Road,   ~~ASHFORD,~~
Balham, S W.   ~~PETERSFIELD~~
18 October 1908

My dear de la Mare,

Don't forget to send me a bit of your story. I should like to see it all but doubt if I should have time. Are you suggesting Beckford? I daresay he will hardly be a big enough <u>name</u> to suit Hutchinson. How would Sir Philip Sidney do? What with history, character & criticism you could make a full & various book. Can I see you next week? — I get back to town on Tuesday. If you are going to be in town any day (except Tuesday) come & have lunch with me. Call at

> 36 Great George St.,
>   Westminster.

Ground floor: 2nd door on right. But I hope you will get away soon & not come in for all winds, rains & frosts.

> Yours ever
> Edward Thomas.

39

Thomas's plan to "see if anything occurs" probably inspired by de la Mare's current freedom to write, results in a series of poetic sketches in early 1909, collected as Rest and Unrest *in 1910.*

13 Rusham Road
Balham. SW.
26 October 1908

My dear de la Mare,

I hope we can meet on Friday, & do let it be lunch if possible. If it can't be, tell me when you are likely to be calling. And could you come to stay with us the week end after this? The week end ticket (Friday to Tuesday or intermediate days) costs 5/9. Send the story when you can. Why should I do Beckford? Why should I do anything? I want to do no books for a time, just to see if anything occurs to me. So far I have never had an opportunity of writing a book I wanted to write — I mean really wanted to whether I had time & payment or not.

Very much hoping to see you on Friday if not before — & with remembrances to your wife & the three

Yours ever
Edward Thomas.

Will you call at 36 Great George St. at 1.15 (or 1) if you can lunch with me?

40

On leaving Anglo-American, de la Mare set himself to write at least two poems a week. He sends the first ones to Thomas. Many of these poems later appear in The Listeners and Other Poems *(1912) and* Peacock Pie: A Book of Rhymes *(1913). Thomas's emphasis on the placing of accented syllables points the way to his own later poetic experiments with speech and metre accents.*
The 'monkey's tale' is de la Mare's The Three Mulla-Mulgars. *He also starts the novel,* The Return.

13 Rusham Road
Balham, S W.
4 November 1908

My dear de la Mare,

I am sorry you have to put off coming especially as it is on account of your wife — I do hope she will soon be really well again & that your fears are disappointed. I have hurried through the poems at once & liked many of them but chiefly

Never-to-be.

An Epitaph
'Be gentle, O hands of a child.'
'No sound over the deep
'Nod'
'Mrs McQueen.'
& rather less: —
The Stranger
'Or to take arms'
After 'The Dynasts'

By the way I never feel sure about your way of dividing up such lines, but I feel sure that in the last verse ("of 'The Dynasts'") it is faulty & you really could write the verse in eight lines

[Seven short lines completely scribbled over follow here]

or in a dozen other ways. But it is lines that end on an unaccented syllable that look really wrong

Still trembling
And still unafraid —
Where burgeons
Soldiers' Asphodel.

I think these pieces are up to all but your very best & you ought to send them out with confidence.

My wife would like to come over & see you both <u>& the children</u>, but she comes so seldom to town that her time may be full up on her possible visit before Christmass. I will let you know later on.

How is the monkey's tale?

Yours ever
Edward Thomas

41

Thomas reviews Davies' New Poems, *which was dedicated to Thomas and his wife, three times in January 1907, in the 3 January* Morning Post, *the 24 January* Daily Chronicle *and the* Bookman. *His review of Davies's* The Autobiography of a Super-tramp *appears in 1908 in the 23 April* Daily Chronicle *and the 14 May* Morning Post. *He later anthologises Davies's*

poem, 'The End of Summer', in the 1916 Flowers I Love *and a character from*
Super-tramp *reappears in Thomas's poem 'Lob'.*
Arthur St John Adcock was the editor of the Bookman.

                                        Llanddensaint
                                        [in pencil, Aug-Dec '08]

My dear de la Mare,
    When you see that I am in Wales you will forgive me for not
coming to see you or arranging to meet in town. I am only here for
a week & shall be in London again on the 24th & soon after that
may I hope to see you. Or is tea on the 24th in town possible? You
suggest time & place & I will be there. Write to me at 13 Rusham
Road, Balham, & I shall hear all right. I am here only for a night.
I am spending all day in walking here & there, seeing mountains &
lakes & collieries, not for the Commission by the way, but because
I like it & London was too much for me. Until now I have forgotten to tell you that Adcock sent me Davies' 'New Poems' after all
because he wanted to economise space by combining the notice of
it with one of the supertramp which I did sometime ago. I am
sorry but you will understand & be sorry too when you see the
wretched four lines devoted to this good book. Adcock ought to
have explained perhaps but I suppose he did not.
    I hope your wife is quite well – tell me — & the children, too.
                            Yours Ever
                            Edward Thomas

                                    42

Thomas's use of spacing highlights the words 'miss you' in the first line of this
letter, emphasised further by the ligatures in 'Iwassorryto'.
Thomas wrote the introduction to Dent's The life and plays of Christopher
Marlowe, *published in 1909.*

                                        13 Rusham Rd
                                        Balham S W.
                                        25 November 1908

My dear de la Mare,
    I was sorry to miss you but I think I said write to Ashford didn't

I? I didn't get here till after midnight on Tuesday & was at the Museum all day. But I had some news of you from Ingpen & was very glad to know your wife is better. I must come over soon but am too busy this week writing about Marlowe. What shall I say? I doubt if my wife will be up for more than one day. Are you likely to be in town tomorrow? If so I could have tea with you at 5 & be free till 6.30. Tell me where or call here: only tell me when you will call as I might be out seeing a doctor, another one.

> In a hurry
> Yours Ever
> Edward Thomas.

43

> 13 R[usham Rd],
> Balham S W..
> 19 November 1908
> [postmarked NO 20 08]

My wife is coming up next week, I expect on Thursday the 10th. Would that evening perhaps suit you? Meantime, could you have tea with me in town next Friday the 4th?

> E.T.

44

As Thomas's 23 February 1909 letter to de la Mare reveals, this letter from Thomas to Bishop helps ensure de la Mare's invitation to the Square Club, a monthly dining club for established younger generation writers, founded by Edward Garnett, G.K. Chesterton and Conal O'Riordan in memory of Mr Square the philosopher in Henry Fielding's novel, Tom Jones. *Its members included J.D. Beresford, John Galsworthy, W.H. Hudson, Roger Ingpen, Edgar Jepsen, John Masefield and Edward Thomas. Later, Ezra Pound also attended.*

> Ashford
> Petersfield.
> 30 December 1908

Dear Bishop,
    Here is de la Mare's first book, & I hope you will like 'Lovelocks'

'John Mouldy' 'Slim Sophia' & many other pieces in it.
    Yours
        Edward Thomas.

45

De la Mare's neighbour, Mr Lintoff, played the violin very badly.
The reference to 'work' suggests paid rather than creative writing.
Thomas has now left the Commission.
The 'stories' are Thomas's Rest and Unrest *sketches.*
De la Mare becomes a regular attendant at Thomas's fortnightly teas at St George's Restaurant in St Martin's Lane with other writerly friends, who later were to include John Freeman, W.H. Davies, Ralph Hodgson and Robert Frost.

        Ashford
        6 January 1909

My dear de la Mare,

    We were sorry you did not come & we are booked for the 16th. Nor am I quite sure yet about the 23rd, but would that suit you? I am coming to town on Tuesday & staying till Thursday morning probably. Are you going to be in town Tuesday or Wednesday at tea time? I shall be in the smoking room at St. George's Restaurant in St Martin's Lane on Tuesday at 5 or so in any case. Suggest a time & place to suit yourself & I will come if I can. I couldn't make out why you expected me to be amused by the fact that you had a neighbour out of his mind & living alone: I know I am callous about most things that don't concern myself, but not amused: what was your point?

    I hope you are all well & that you have work & can do it. I am without work & am writing stories without events, queer dull, sombre, languid things which nobody will ever print or see.

    Yours Ever
        Edward Thomas

46

Thomas discusses arrangements for de la Mare's first visit to Berryfield Cottage.
De la Mare described how his bedroom at Thomas's was so cold that he could hardly hold the pen between his fingers.

Thomas uses unorthodox spacing to emphasis the "room" de la Mare will have to work in.
Thomas's Jefferies *is receiving good reviews.*
De la Mare had borrowed Thomas's Wales.

> BERRYFIELD COTTAGE,
> ASHFORD,
> PETERSFIELD.
> 18 January 1909

My dear de la Mare,

Which train will you come by on Saturday? There is the 9.5 from Waterloo & the 3.40, also the 2.40 which you can catch at Clapham junction at 2.49. The week end ticket costs 5/9 from Waterloo & 5/6 from Clapham junction. I hope you will stay till Tuesday. You will have a room with a fire & a table (& a piano) so that you can read & write if you like. Please bring 'Wales' with you at last. Aren't you glad you don't write for a paper that thinks it is doing a kind act by describing you as 'Mr Edward Thomas a better writer than Richard Jefferies… '? God forgive them & preserve me from them. I hope all of you will Remember us both, & will your wife let you bring one of the children down with you? We should all like it.

> Yours Ever
> Edward Thomas.

47

Thomas praises de la Mare's The Three Mulla-Mulgars, *describing it later in an 8 December 1910* Morning Post *review as "a happy and perfect inspiration".*
Thomas reviewed Alfred Noyes's Drake: An English Epic *in the 5 October 1909* Morning Post *and includes Noyes's 'Song' in* The Pocket Book.

> Ashford
> Petersfield.
> 1 February 1909

My dear de la Mare,

Here is your M.S. I only read on another 5 or 6 pages or so being busy & also finding the reading very slow. But I should think there is no doubt it will be a very good thing altogether. Personally I like it very much & I also think it stands a good chance of being

understood & enjoyed by a great many people – old & very young.
I only wish I could recommend it to some publisher with success.
Have you thought of anyone?

I go to town tomorrow but only for one day & night as I don't
want to interrupt my work so I can't see you this time.

Jefferies is out & begins to get the kind of treatment its vague-
ness & insufficiency deserves, but so far the treatment is kindly. I
rank with Noyes except that I write better.

Yours ever
Edward Thomas

48

Thomas provides de la Mare with a precious opportunity of meeting writers
and editors by inviting him into the Square Club.
Thomas's 30 December 1908 letter clearly convinced Bishop to invite de la
Mare to the club.
R.A. Scott-James was literary editor of the Daily News *at this time.*

Ashford
23 February 1909

Dear de la Mare,

Will you join the Square Club? You pay 1/. a year to cover the
cost of sending out invitations & the dinner costs 3/6. Do if you
can. Bishop wants me to ask you. [Scott-J?] I know would be glad
to see you there & I think it might be useful, too.

Let me know & then I will tell Bishop & he will warn you of the
next meeting (which is to be on the 27th of March, I think).

Yours ever
Edward Thomas.

49

The opening lines of the letter refer to the Square Club.
Thomas's reference to being "servantless" and his description of birds scrab-
bling for crumbs suggest his own lack of earnings at this time.
The stories are Thomas's Rest and Unrest *sketches.*

BERRYFIELD COTTAGE,
ASHFORD,
PETERSFIELD.
1 March 1909

My dear de la Mare,

There could not be & there are not any dissentients. There are no formalities. Also, frankly, we do want more members. So I will assume you will be one of us & hope to see you on the 23rd or whenever it is. But I shall see you before, I hope. I shall be in town one night next week, probably. Might I come to you then, on the evening of the 9th? My wife can't come I am afraid. We are servantless & everything is in rather a mess. But by the way if you want to see snow come this very day, will you? If you turn up at any time we shall welcome you. I wish the snow would go for the birds, thousands of them, are wretched at our doors & the more food we give the more come, & there is just as little for each as if we only threw out our table crumbs. I will bring stories with me next week if I get the typewritten copies in time.

In a hurry, with our love to you all

Ever yours
Edward Thomas.

50

BERRYFIELD COTTAGE,
ASHFORD,
PETERSFIELD.
5 March 1909

Dear de la Mare

Here are four of my latest sketchs [sic]. Will you look at them & let me have them back when I come on Tuesday, or if you can't have me on Tuesday please send them so as to reach me on Wednesday morning at

13 Rusham Road,
Nightingale Lane
S.W.

In great haste
Yours ever
Edward Thomas.

51

1 April 1909

I can't manage Wednesday, but hope to see you on Tuesday in smoking room at St George's Restaurant a little after 4.30 – I <u>might</u> be free to come on to supper, if you will let me take pot luck.
E.T..

52

The lack of gaps in Thomas's ligatured "I am so full of work" humorously enacts his sense of lack of time.
Harry Hooton is one of Thomas's oldest friends and attends Thomas's fortnightly meetings at St George's restaurant in St Martin's Lane.
Thomas Seccombe's Times Literary Supplement *review of Jefferies comes out on 2 April 1909, thus helping to date this letter.*

[in pencil 1909?]

My dear de la Mare,
    I can't come on Tuesday. I am only up two nights, first for the Square Club & second at a friend's who asked me early in the month. And I daren't stay longer I amsofull of work. So where can we meet? Outside Eustace Miles at 4 on Monday or 4.30 on Tuesday? You can't reply in time now for Monday so I will be there in any case, also on Tuesday unless I hear to the contrary at
        13 Rusham Rd
        Balham S W..
Try to make it Monday as I have more time then. My wife would have liked nothing better in town than to see you all again but she is bound here especially as we are at present without a maid.
    Bring Hooton on Monday or Tuesday if you can find him – I don't know where he is.
    My reviews have been very favourable. The best so far was Garnett's in the Daily News. He is quite pleased with the book. The Times was kind too – Seccombe's I should say.
        Till Monday Goodbye.
            Yours ever
            Edward Thomas.

53

Thomas and de la Mare provide mutual support for each other during periods
of depression and physical ill health.
Thomas is beginning to value himself more as a writer.
The work in a box is probably further sketches, although some have already
been sent out to editors.
Mervyn is Thomas's son.

> BERRYFIELD COTTAGE,
> ASHFIELD,
> PETERSFIELD.
> 11 May 1909

My dear de la Mare,

I was sorry to miss you, but hope to see you at the Square Club Thursday week, the 20th — don't forget. I hope your headache is better now. What a pity you aren't here this fine weather enjoying it as I do not know how to. I am not up to much but creep along hoping that it will not always be quite so bad, knowing it in fact. I go on writing & then putting what I write into a box. Work does not abound & I am refusing what is offered because I will not take low prices for what I don't really want to do. May I see your rhymes?

Will you come down this Summer anytime you like? I mean this literally (but am to be away from home between May 25 & about June 7).

I don't know when I can come again to see you. Now Mervyn is at school my wife will hardly get to town for a while.

> Yours ever
> Edward Thomas.

54

> BERRYFORD COTTAGE,
> ASHFORD,
> PETERSFIELD.
> [in pencil, before 25 May 1909?]

My dear de la Mare,

As I can't get to town at a convenient time this month to see

you, & am shortly leaving, won't you come down on Sunday next?
I believe there is a cheap ticket to Petersfield every Sunday by an
early train. If you can come, find out the time of arrival & I will
meet you. I think it is 3/6. I am very busy & have been, or I would
have written or seen you before now.

Ever yours

Edward Thomas.

55

Thomas had praised Pound's Personae *as "hard, naked, and grim".*
Many of de la Mare's poems mentioned in this letter appear in The Listeners
and Peacock Pie *with Thomas's revisions in place.*
*Thomas's criticisms of de la Mare's archaisms echo his similar criticisms of
Pound in a 7 June 1909* Daily Chronicle *review.*
*Thomas's focus on de la Mare's over-repetition of words and consonants
highlights his own reliance on the sound of the line or phrase or rhyme as a
guide to redrafting. His comments also illuminate his later thinking behind the
ordering of his 1917* Poems.
*In her life of de la Mare, Theresa Whistler records that his children christened
the garden at their Anerley home 'Tim and Bill's Orchard'.*
Hueffer, later known as Ford Madox Ford, is editor of the English Review.
The Synge play is The Playboy of the Western World. *Thomas had reviewed
it in 1907 in the August* Bookman *and the 13 September* Daily Chronicle.

BERRYFIELD COTTAGE,
ASHFORD,
PETERSFIELD.
8 June 1909

My dear de la Mare,

I feel unusually foolish in writing about poetry today as I have
just made the most horrible mistakes in saying — in the
'Chronicle' yesterday & also in 'The English Review' — that Ezra
Pound is a poet. He is not & how I came to mesmerise myself into
praising him I can't think. I began by thinking his work rot but so
contemptuously that I seem to have set about altering my view out
of pure perversity & desire to be amiable.

Nevertheless this is to say I liked almost all of these poems very
much & even more than I hoped I could. Except 'The Fiddler',
'King David' & 'Arabia' & 'The Three Kings' I liked them all &

especially those which I have ticked in the contents. Forgive my making the briefest remarks as it is late & I am tired.

I doubt if it is wise to have Nos. 2, 3, 4, 5, 6, 7, 8 & 10 close together as they are very closely alike in effect, but of this I am not sure. They are peculiarly to my taste & I like each one better than the rest as I read it!

'Old Ben'   – ? do you mean the surname to be so spelt.
                     ? The last verse, especially the last 2 lines, don't seem quite right.

'Old Susan' – ? are you satisfied with 'absorbed & sage'

'Miss Sims' – ? I am not sure about the phrase 'Phantoms of the Unseen' in its context.

'The Picture'– lines 10 & 11 the repetition of 'green' is ineffective & might be avoided.

'The Grange' line 8. I don't like the 'breeZE STirs' & should prefer 'breath' or 'puff'.
                     line 11. 'gone's noon' is unnecessarily whimsical, praps.

'The Angel' – line 1, did you mean 'no one were'?

'Nod'   line 17 I didn't like 'molied' & thought of simply using the substantive 'moly' but it might suggest then 'covered with moles'.

'Mockery'   line 14, is 'when it's echo o'er' permissible?

'Arabia'   lines 4-8 I don't understand

'Truants'   lines 9 & 10 & especially 10 seemed unworthy. Could you spare the verse?

'The Tired Cupid' line 19 'surge' is too formidable & line 23-4 I won't have 'dew-bediamon'd'.

'Keys of Morning' 33 & 34 the two 'withs' are clumsy & there is a relative pronoun elided not very satisfactorily.

'The Witch' 8th verse is weak in itself & does not appear to be essential.

'The Two Children' last verse, do you like the rhyme of lines 1 & 2

'Music Unheard' I shouldn't like to touch this, but I hesitated at 'Disquiet of' (lines 3 & 4, 3rd verse) & thought of 'Disquiet with' though the sound is inferior.

For Hueffer I should suggest any of the first 10, or 'Bill & Jim's Orchard,' or 'Nod', or 'The Truants' or 'The Three Cherry Trees' & 'Music Unheard'. 'Rachel' I do not see. All those I like best belong rather to 'Songs of Childhood' than 'Poems', don't they? I think they are equal to the best you have written & they ought to be made into a book. I would introduce them to Elkin Mathews if you you [sic] like. He would only offer a royalty, but would (I hope) publish at his own risk.

I hope we shall see you on Friday. We may go to see a play of J.M. Synge's on Saturday afternoon at 'The Court'. If so, could you join us there?
Yours ever
Edward Thomas.

56

De la Mare and his family spend a month's holiday at Dene Cottage in West Harting, a four or five mile walk from Thomas's place. This was to become a regular summer holiday home.
De la Mare liked to work outside there, writing under a tree.
Thomas encourages de la Mare to take longer walks than was his usual custom.
The de la Mare and Thomas families see each other often. On 16 July Thomas tells Bottomley of his delight in de la Mare's "singularly (sometimes comically) restless & curious & innocent mind."
Bronwen is Thomas's elder daughter.

Saturday.
[in pencil, July [11 deleted] 10 [?] 1909]

My dear de la Mare,
    Do come over if ever you feel inclined to stay a night. I hope you re better now. I expect I shall come on the Monday or Tuesday & then later in the week bring Bronwen. If you let me know when you will Reach Petersfield, say the Post Office at the Harting end of the High Street, next to 'The Dolphin', I will meet you there. Or if on the other hand you could be there at 3.15 on Monday we could walk back to your place, unless you would come back with me & stay a night.
    It is grand weather for Pique's Slugs.

I write in sight of your little fir wood & wish I could attract your attention.

We did enjoy Thursday's visit.

Yours ever
    Edward Thomas

57

The next few letters discuss Thomas's Rest and Unrest. *Despite the quick turn-around Thomas demands, de la Mare is not simply proof-reading but also making suggestions of improvements that Thomas then takes up.*

Thomas, a prodigious walker, encourages de la Mare to take extended walks with him.

Geoffrey Lupton, a furniture-maker, is building for Thomas and his family a home that conforms to William Morris designs on his land on the top of Ashford Hanger.

> BERRYFIELD COTTAGE,
> ASHFORD,
> PETERSFIELD.
> 16 September 1909

My dear de la Mare,

The proofs of my little book of sketches have just begun to come in. I wonder would you read them for me? As you have not seen most of them I thought you might be willing to. On the chance that you are, I enclose the first batch. As they are so small perhaps you could return them the day after receiving them? They ought to be got through quickly as the sooner the book is out the better. Shall I see you at the Square Club next week? I suppose it is Wednesday the 22nd, tho the card said Tuesday the 22nd. I should like to come to Anerley on the Tuesday coming but doubt if I can manage it. Supposing that evening is convenient to you I will let you know if I can manage it.

About a walk – my walk with Lupton is off. If we do get some promising weather soon are you prepared to come here at once & start a walk? Or would you rather start from London? I would snatch 3 or 4 days if you could come. Suppose you come down here in any case on the 24th next week, taking a week end (which lasts to the 28th). Then if fine we would start off either on the Friday evening or Saturday morning & do a circuit, ending here

on Tuesday in time for you to get back that night. Think of it.
 Yours Ever with our love to you all
  Edward Thomas

58

The new house includes a separate study cottage for Thomas, which was available for use from April 1909.
Thomas continues the discussion of Rest and Unrest.

  Ashford
  19 September 1909

My dear de la Mare,

 Thank you for your praise & for your suggestions — I have adopted all but one & that because I do not want to make the corrections too heavy. I know I write carelessly, partly in contempt for my own finical ways, partly in haste, partly out of the weakness of the flesh. I ought to have seen these faults myself & am very gratified to you for pointing them out.

 What a pity we aren't walking <u>now</u>. Yesterday & today are quite perfect Autumn days. Do think about next week end <u>independently</u> of <u>weather</u>. You can have my study in the old house for as many hours as you like. Try, & perhaps you could bring one of the children. We should all be glad of one or more or you, but especially you. Our love to you all & condolences for the big toe of Pickles. I will look for you on Tuesday then, also (probably) Wednesday, at St Georges between 4 & 5.

  Yours Ever
  Edward Thomas.

59

'At a Cottage Door' appears in Rest and Unrest, *where "with" replaces "by" in the sentence discussed here.*

  [in pencil, after 22 September 1909]

My dear de la Mare,

 Thank you for proofs of A Cottage Door. I agree with you in nearly every case,★ specially that one sentence in the soliloquy^. I expect the 2nd lot I sent you will be back by the noon post but I want to send you a word now in case you can meet me on Monday. I won't come over in the evening because it means staying out late & smoking a lot & I have had a very bad time all this week attributable, if to any thing, to the Square Club evening. I am sorry but I cannot risk being upset in this way & it is not only I that suffer. Well, suppose you meet me on Monday outside Eustace Miles at 1 or at 4. You have no time to reply, so I will be there in any case. I hope you can come.

> Yours ever
> E T.

* I have altered it to 'tangled up & darkened by a number of things' or something like that.
^ which I had not failed to notice myself

60

'The Maiden's Wood' and 'Snow and Sand' appear in Rest and Unrest.

> Ashford
> Petersfield.
> 5 October 1909

My dear de la Mare,

Here is the end. I now perceive for the first time – it is inconceivable folly – that 'The Maiden's Wood' has no end, & that 'Snow & Sand' could have been cleaned up in several places. It is too late. On the whole I feel most of these things are presentable of their kind but the Lord does not grant me the power to see what kind that is — which may be mercy but is not justice.

> Yours ever
> Edward Thomas.

61

With the help of de la Mare's close criticism of his sketches, Thomas begins to review his own writing processes. This leads on to his 1913 experiments with The Childhood of Edward Thomas *in writing recollections of his life without adding, interpreting or inventing anything.*

Thomas's interest in houses continues into his poetry, many of which feature houses.

'The Island', 'Winter Music' and 'The Castle of Lostormellyn' in Thomas's 1911 Light and Twilight *all draw on Welsh legend. 'The Castle of Lostormellyn' appeared in the* Tramp *in June 1910. De la Mare is now discussing Thomas's reviews on a more equal basis, as a reviewer himself.*

Ashford
9 October 1909

My dear de la Mare,

Many thanks for your letter and the proofs — & for your excuses for my inconclusiveness. There may be excuses for inconclusiveness. But not for negligence. I didn't realise, till I saw these in print, what a hurry I had been in. Probably at the back of it all is my notebook habit. Either I must overcome that or I must write much more laboriously — not mix the methods of more or less intuitive writing & of slaving adding bits of colour & so on. Bottomley sternly advises me to burn my notebooks & buy no more. I doubt if I should obey, even if I knew he was right & that it was worth so much pains to be right! You are right about Symons, I mean about my review. I knew I was not just, though right, up to a point; but I had no time to revise. For I was in the thick of another study of a house. I must try to avoid drifting into writing that merely gives me an excuse for my most obvious characteristics. I am thinking of some old Welsh legends. To handle things so detached in <u>form</u> would compel me to be more careful.

It was so fine this morning & last night that I was going to write to ask you to come down, but thought you probably would not at such short notice. But it is quite likely that next week will be fine. If Monday or Tuesday is promising, will you come? We shall not need any notice. We will keep a supply of vinegar at hand. But if you know it is impossible to come some time next week send me a postcard & then I can set off for a walk if I feel inclined.

    I hope you are all well,
      Yours ever
        Edward Thomas.

62

Florence and Dick are de la Mare's two oldest children.
De la Mare and Thomas share books and experiences as fellow reviewers.
Thomas reviews Brock's book on Shelley in the December 1909 Bookman.

Ashford
14 October 1909

My dear de la Mare,

I got a prize for handwriting when I was 13, so there. I am sorry you haven't come down. Today has been perfect. If it lasts why not come down on Saturday & stay till I go up to town on Tuesday; & bring Florence or Dick — now do. I shall be at St George's on Tuesday at 4 or so, but hope to see you before then.

Alas, I could not say all I feel about Kipling in the Saturday Review. I should have been taken for a little Englander. But it looks as if they are not going to print the review as no proof has come.

After wasting 4 hours on Max Beerbohm's 'Yet Again' I have had to return it to the Morning Post. Have you had it?

I am sending Brock's 'Shelley'. He tells us what Shelley ought to have done & ought not.

Yours ever
Edward Thomas.

63

Thomas's exhilaration at moving to his new house in Wick Green comes through in this letter.
J.B. Pinker, de la Mare's agent, is trying to place The Three Mulla-Mulgars, *eventually published by Duckworth in 1910 after enthusiastic recommendation by their reader, Edward Garnett, in September 1909.*
Ford Madox Hueffer published de la Mare's short story, 'The Almond Tree', in the August English Review.
Thomas wrote The Heart of England *in 1906.*
Every week Hudson and Garnett met with literary friends for lunch at the Mont Blanc restaurant in Gerrard Street in London. These included Thomas Seccombe, R.A. Scott-James, Stephen Reynolds, W.H. Davies, Hilaire Belloc, Muirhead Bone, Ford Madox Hueffer, Perceval Gibbon, John Galsworthy and occasionally Joseph Conrad.

Ashford
30 November 1909

My dear de la Mare,

I was meaning to write to you – or to your wife to enquire delicately if you were still alive. It is very good news that you are. I wish you were nearer. We move to

Week Green
nr Petersfield

on the 18th & I wish you would come & stay with us soon. Perhaps you will find the hill top better for you. We I hope shall be the same at the hill top as at the bottom I was sorry to hear you were not well & Dick ill. We have all been well except that Mervyn has a stupid cough which does not keep him in or hurt his spirits, though. We have been very busy indeed gardening in the fine weather. I didn't much like it but it did me good. Work for the paper has been very slack. The Chronicle treats me badly & the Morning Post has practically dropped me — I fancy there are changes there. So I am not in the best position. However, I have done some other writing lately — another house & family group, partly from memory, & so on. So far I have not got a book to do. Has Pinker any news of the Mullah-mullahs? Mann, the new member of the Square, was telling me how much he liked 'The Almond Tree.' By the way, they say the English Review is on its last legs.

I am coming up next week. Can you be at St George's on Tuesday at 4? You might like to come to the Mont Blanc at Gerrard Street at 1.30.

Have you a copy of Drayton? I have a good selection you might like. It is among a few duplicates I don't need to take up to the new house. Would you like a copy of 'The Heart of England'?

I wish you lived near.

With our love to you all & especially Dick.

By the way have the children got a book of birds or of flowers? I mean can they do with another. I have one of each to spare, if you let me know soon.

Yours Ever
Edward Thomas.

64

De la Mare and Thomas both read de la Mare's poetry to their children.
Thomas later reads them his own stories in Four-and-Twenty Blackbirds.

WEEK GREEN,
PETERSFIELD.
29 December 1909

My dear de la Mare,

I am called up to town suddenly & so shall be at St George's to tea tomorrow (Thursday) — can you be there at 4? Hooton also is up, & I have asked him to be there. I am very much worried & hurried today so will not write, but how good the old Jay's verses are! I liked some enormously & the children, too. They will write to you.

Yours ever
Edward Thomas

P.S. I think I could get down to Anerley with you afterwards if you were free, but there will be no way of getting at me unless we meet at St George's first. So can you come prepared to take me back to pot luck — no peacocks, by request.

65

Ralph Hodgson was a popular poet and a good friend of Thomas's.
Thomas's care for and encouragement of poet friends he admires is reflected by his reviews of Davies's Farewell to Poesy *this year – covered in the 28 March* Daily Chronicle, *the 7 April* Morning Post *and the May 1910* Bookman *where the review is entitled 'The Natural Poet'.*

24 March 1910

My dear de la Mare,

The Editor of the country magazine I told you about would be glad to see any poems of yours which would not be unsuitable in subject. You know what I mean. If you like send me a few to choose from. If you have two or three you feel are possible send them to
Ralph Hodgson

c/o Cassell & Co
La Belle Sauvage   EC.
Ludgate Hill.
He wants to print 2 poems & Davies is likely to do one. He has had 100s sent in. Send as soon as possible.
Yours Ever
Edward Thomas

66

Thomas is researching for a book on poetic inspiration, Feminine Influence on the Poets *and preparing for the writing of his critical biography on Maeterlinck.*
In 1909 Ella Coltman, companion of Henry and Margaret Newbolt, gave de la Mare a life subscription to the London Library, which he now shares with Thomas.

Wick ~~WEEK~~ GREEN,
PETERSFIELD.
5 April 1910

My dear de la Mare.

Did you get a card from me a fortnight ago recommending you to send some verses to Ralph Hodgson c/o Cassells, La Belle Sauvage? In case you didn't, I will repeat that he would like to see some things of yours that would not obviously look uncomfortable in a magazine called 'Outdoor Life'. He has taken a poem by Davies. Don't answer this. I come up Wednesday next week just for the day. Will you be at St George's at 4? I am very busy all day now, working & gardening. So I shall be glad of a week end with you here. When will you come? Any week end will suit us now -- this next one or any other. Come when you can. If you could bring with you Gosse's 'Seventeenth Century Studies' I should be glad. That book called 'Femmes Inspiratrices et Poètes Annonciateurs' was almost useless, by the way. It only related to one or two special cases & the writer is not very intelligent besides being a little crazed.

I hope you are all well,
Yours Ever
Edward Thomas.

67

De la Mare and his family are to spend August near Thomas in Dene Cottage,
West Harting.
Goodwood horse races.

Wick
~~WEEK~~ GREEN,
PETERSFIELD.
9 April 1910

My dear de la Mare,

Thanks for the book & list. May I have Finck's 'Romantic Love'
& Rousselot's 'L'Histoire de problème de l'amour en moyen age'?
I will return the books I have on Wednesday. Also then I hope you
will have fixed on a week end to suit yourself, as at present any one
suits us — remember this. Your news about August is very good.
We must try to get an easy walk sometime then & pay our respects
to Goodwood (first week in August or thereabouts) on our way.

Our love to you all & we wish you lived at Steep. St Georges at
4 on Wednesday.

      Yours ever
        Edward Thomas.

P.S. The Anthology I was thinking of is by Anita Bartle & consists
of poems & c about & to the Virgin, but I can't recall the title.
Could you perhaps lend me this also?

What a brilliant book Sichel's Sterne is.

68

De la Mare had sent Hodgson the poem 'The Three Cherry Trees', later
published in The Listeners *1912. Thomas quoted it in his August 1912*
Bookman *review and* In Pursuit of Spring, *1914. He also anthologised it in*
Flowers I Love, *1916. His 8 June 1909 letter to de la Mare records his initial*
response to the poem.
Mervyn was visiting Thomas's parents in Balham.

Wick ~~WEEK~~ GREEN
PETERSFIELD.
24 April 1910

My dear de la Mare,

Will you let me know your train on Friday & also when it leaves Waterloo or Clapham Junction? Mervyn is returning home on Friday & I should be grateful if you would accept him as a companion. He could join you at Clapham Junction if you look out for him.

I met Ralph Hodgson on Friday & he was admiring a poem of yours <u>repeating it by heart</u> which is more than I can do but there was one delicious verse about the lady who was 'by far the most fair'. Unhappily the magazine is going to die before birth, so I suppose you will have the poem back.

Can you bring down with you any of the following books? —

1 Dowden's Shelley
2 Vol. 2 in Blackwood's Periods of English Literature, i.e. 'The Flourishing of Romance & the Rise of Allegory' by Saintsbury
3 S. Gwynn's 'Thomas Moore' in English Men of Letters.

I look forward to your coming. Do not fail or this bl–dy book will drive me silly — I wish it <u>would</u> drive me <u>mad.</u>
      Yours ever
       Edward Thomas.

We expected you at the Blue Bird & wasted a ticket.

69

This month de la Mare mentions to his agent, J.B. Pinker, that he is writing "twenty to thirty simple rhymes in a day", probably intended for A Child's Day, *a portfolio of child's photographs and rhymes, described by de la Mare to* Saturday Westminster Gazette *literary editor Naomi Royde-Smith as "this ghastly doggerel" in July 1912.*
On 24 July 1910 Thomas writes to Bottomley that de la Mare "is doing very good work now, some of it very happy childish rhyming, most delicate & new."

[postmarked AP 27 10]

Would you send word straight through to Mervyn about the time of the train? He is at 13 Rusham Rd, Balham. This is in case you have not already written to me.

Many thanks for your letter & the poems. I will not write as you are coming so soon, but I will look at the poems before then. I am hoping to hear that you can meet Mervyn. My mother will probably take him to the station, & he will wear a red cap. If you arrive at Petersfield before 5.30 your things will be taken up, so I hope you will.   E.T.

70

A probable reference to de la Mare's poem, 'Longlegs', later published in Peacock Pie, *an affectionate poem about Thomas.*

[postmarked MY 8 10]

Can you send on Frank Harris's book on Shakespeare if you are at the Library on Monday or Tuesday?

Sunday

I am going to be in town tomorrow & Tuesday but am prevented from making certain arrangements. So I want you to come to St George's unless you happen to be near. I shall be there between 4 & 6 on either day & perhaps both, or on Tuesday rather earlier.

Longlegs

71

Wick   ~~WEEK~~ GREEN
PETERSFIELD
[in pencil 1910 - 11?]

My dear de la Mare,

I am very sorry indeed that I missed you on Tuesday last. I got to St Georges at 4.5 & stayed till just on 4.35 & then I left & caught the 4.55 home, making sure you were not coming. It shall not occur again, though doubtless you will be uppish from your connection with Melville. What is the Jewish form of Melville, as Levi is of Lee?

Can you be at St Georges next Tuesday before the Square dinner at 4? I am asking Hodgson & someone else to come & meet you so do come.

I hope you are all well & liking this weather. You should have been here.

If Harris' book can be had fairly soon I would very much like it. If not I must see it at the Museum. I am bringing back Dowden with me – what invertebrate sweet slush it is.

> Yours ever
> Edward Thomas.

72

De la Mare admired Davies's work and was attracted by his unusual character, writing to Newbolt on 2 July that there "never could have been a more delightfully clear view of the world seen by one man, as [sic] his."
The "troublesome book" is Feminine Influence on the Poets.

> WEEK GREEN
> PETERSFIELD
> 12 June 1910

My dear de la Mare,

I want you to do without me on Tuesday week, the 21st. If I were to stay as long as I wanted to, I should be too tired & that I dare not be after a recent experience. I had already arranged to bring Davies, but am asking Hooton now to bring him instead. I am going to take a few days walking from about the 21st to the 27th. There might then be some hope of getting my head clear — perhaps empty – for this troublesome book. I hope you will not mind: there is nothing in town I should like better than spending an evening with you, but I am really not fit for any fatigue in London just yet. I hope Dick is getting well & the others not getting ill. With our love

> Yours ever
> Edward Thomas.

73

Thomas's youngest daughter, Myfanwy, was born on 16 August 1910.

> Wick ~~WEEK~~ GREEN
> PETERSFIELD
> 27 July 1910

My dear de la Mare,

Bronwen & I will be coming over on Saturday afternoon if that suits you. We shall start from here about 2 & be at Goose Green a little before 4. You are missing Goodwood. Friday is the last day & I suppose you can't come then? If by any chance you can, of course do. I may be going that day. With our love (we are still only four)

Yours ever

Edward Thomas

P.S. It has occurred to me Bronwen & I can get a lift in the morning & reach you before 10 if that is not too early.

74

The 'Saturday' is probably the Saturday Westminster Gazette. *Its literary editor, Naomi Royde-Smith, was sending de la Mare regular and frequent work.*

WICK GREEN
PETERSFIELD
30 July 1910

My dear de la Mare,

I hope all goes well as it ought to do in this fine weather. I must take Mervyn home next week, so I wonder if when you are coming to town on Tuesday (as I hope you are) you will drop him at Wandsworth Common whence he can go to my mother's & wait for me. If this is convenient don't trouble to write to me but you might send my mother a card — or Mervyn might – saying about when he will arrive. I have just got back from Hodgson's very tired of something & sick & furious with Everything, but nevertheless try to give my love to the five children. So glad the 'Saturday' is promising.

Yours ever Edward Thomas.

75

De la Mare's family were staying at Harting during August.

Friday: Raining.
[postmarked AU 5 10]

We still hope you may come tonight. If not I shall walk over tomorrow morning, arriving about eleven & then take Bronwen home in the afternoon in time for tea. Could you walk back with us & then I will walk home with you on Sunday?   ET.

76

[postmarked AU 15 10]

Things are not quite certain & I may not be able to come tomorrow but I will try to come either in the morning by about midday or in the afternoon.   E.T.

77

Ernest Rhys was founder editor of Dent's Everyman's Library series of affordable classics. He also wrote essays, stories, poetry, novels and plays.

[postmarked AU 25 10]

I am coming over on Friday afternoon & want you to come back with me for a night. The next day you might like to come with me to see Ernest Rhys who is now staying at Berryfield. All well here.
E.T.

78

The proofs are of Feminine Influence on the Poets.

TALBOT HOTEL
TREGARON.
7 September 1910

My dear de la Mare,
    Will you meet me outside the Villa Villa Restaurant in Gerrard Street on Tuesday at 1.30 or a little after? I reach Paddington at 1

& shall come straight on. If you can't, then I shall be at St George's at 4 & have asked Hodgson & will probably bring Davies. I hope you have got some work now & feel able to do it. I have only corrected proofs here & remembered my sins. No books seem to come to me for review at all. Still I have had almost nothing but fine warm weather & have been alone all day in the kind of country I like & so I shan't begin to worry till I am in the train for Petersfield. After Friday I shall be at

    c/o John Williams
      Waun Wen School
        Swansea.

I hear Mervyn & Bronwen had a very good time at West Harting. I wish we were nearer. Do you really want a house nearby? If so probably you would like to be within a mile or two of Petersfield, or what are your plans for schools? With my love to you all

    Yours ever
    Edward Thomas.

79

An insight into the ways writers of this time worked together, reviewing each other's books.
The three books are Maeterlinck, The Icknield Way *and* Lafcadio Hearn.
Thomas reviewed The Three Mulla-Mulgars *in the 8 December* Morning Post, *the 14 December* Daily Chronicle, *and the December* Bookman.

        Wick Green
        22 September 1910

My dear de la Mare,

    I am sorry I forgot the Clare, but it shall go off today. I shall be up next week. Will you meet me outside the Villa Villa at 1.30 on Tuesday? I hope Hudson will be there. If you can't be, come to St George's at 3.30 if possible. I am going to be very busy soon I believe. 3 books to write, worst of all Maeterlinck. Have you begun to get review books again? 'The New Laocoon' is worth reading & look out for Hudson's new book, 'A Shepherd's Life.' Let me know a few days beforehand when to expect your Mulgars. The novel it is no use my asking for except at the Bookman, & there you are sure of a friendly notice. — all well here. My wife is nearly herself again. Baby weighs 13lbs & is named Helen Elizabeth Myvanwy. It is lovely here now these misty sunlit days. You ought to be here. By the way you did not say whether you seriously thought the neighbourhood of Petersfield possible — I wish you did. Hooton is moving to Coulsdon soon & is lodging now at Croydon. Our five loves to you all

      Ever yours

      Edward Thomas

80

Probably in part a response to de la Mare's tender review of Thomas's Rest and Unrest *in the 3 October 1910* Times Literary Supplement: *"a pure delicate prose" and "the work of a mind as sensitive to beauty as a child, and as consciously critical of beauty as an adult".*

Thomas's December 1910 Bookman *'Gallery' feature of de la Mare says he "nourishes [...] a curiosity, a discontent, and an optimism all equally boundless" and is "always original and instructive, and producing effects beyond his calculation and probably beyond our explanation".*

[postmarked OCT 10 10]

I hope you will come to lunch. If not be at St George's early as we had better leave early, hadn't we? I am writing on Walter de la Mare for the Xmas number of the Bookman.

      E.T.

81

Thomas wrote a muted review of The Return *in the December* Bookman. *Although "an honest and brilliant book", the second half is "as fascinating as it is uneventful". Thomas's choice of examples mainly relating to speech or dialogue are perhaps early indications of his later appreciation of the accents of speech in his own poetry. On page 292 of the 1910 edition of* The Return, *Craik's circumlocutory speech is set next to an apt and concise descriptive phrase, "he peered largely", and then followed by an amusing reduction of his words by another character.*

The phrase "some things I want to do" could refer to the sketches collected in Light and Twilight *in 1911, many of which were earlier published in the* Nation, *the* Thrush, *the* Tramp *and* English Review.

The visit to Cambridge was to see Rupert Brooke, who had visited Thomas earlier in the year.

Wick Green
Petersfield.
18 October 1910

My dear de la Mare,

I ought to have written to you on Saturday when I finished 'The Return', but I have kept on trying to get a really comfortable hour to write in & now the nearest approach is the half hour I spend trying to keep awake before going to bed. You know I never quite got hold of the book from the parts you read to me & told me about & I think you suspected I was going to be bored. But I enjoyed every bit of it & especially the last half beginning with the introduction of the Herberts. You have put yourself under several great disadvantages 1 in choosing such a character as Lawford 2 in avoiding extraordinary or startling incidents 3 in avoiding farce. I should have thought this meant a severe task but from the uniform goodness of the writing I conclude it was not. Sheila is the best character. She is very good: you give her a lot to do & I always feel you are right about her — except possibly in that final gathering when Lawford listens. I see I have marked the book about page 126 & again from 148 onwards for twenty pages or so as seeming particularly good. Lawford's changes — almost leaps – of character in his capacity of Sabathier are sometimes astonishingly good, e.g. his taking of the idea of Dr Ferguson & in some of his playfulness with Sheila and Miss Sinnett. Perhaps you overdo his weariness on the whole? Looking back I can't see why he should always be so. Bethany is often good – e.g. on p. 185 – but I admit I was surprised when you said he was over 70. Herbert I like; Grisel sometimes I more than like, but was never sure of her age, & in the end she puzzles me (on a first reading) at p.229 & altogether in her determined pouting & the sacramental last day. Craik (especially on p.292) is good, but I felt Danton's treatment was exceptional & inharmonious especially in the conclusion. I must read the last half or so again because I think I may have missed something which would help me to understand Lawford-Sabathier's return to a Lawford recognizable by Miss Sinnet. He is not the old Lawford on p.250 for example, or are you allowing him to be permanently enriched by being Sabathiered without the handicap of looking like a bird of prey? I like all your descriptions of moods & moody scenes — the churchyard, and the house seen from outside, the Herberts' house. Altogether it is a success, a real triumph. But a devil of a book for reviewers, I should say. I haven't tried yet, but shall do for 'The Bookman' if you will <u>ask</u> Arnold to send a copy there, which he will not do as a matter of course, it seems.

I am horribly busy reading & reading & trying to get free to write some things I want to do. I wish I were not going to Cambridge on Friday. However I do look forward to seeing you on my way back on Tuesday — will you be at the Villa Villa at 1.30 & if not at St Georges at 3.30? Tuesday next week. I will ask Hodgson.

Isn't that book on Goldsmith good? I mean so lively and in its way masterly & evidently a work of pleasure — I contrast it with the sort of book on Goldsmith one would expect from Methuens.

Will you come down here before long? Your own time: only don't put it off too long. I wish your wife would come, preferably with you, but alone if that is the only way. My wife is getting on well now. The apples were very good. I ate most but did give the children a taste. They would send their love – if they were not asleep – with mine.   Yours ever
ET.

82

Thomas praises The Three Mulla-Mulgars *highly in the December 1910* Bookman.
De la Mare had sent Thomas a collection of his latest poems.
'The Three Cherry Trees', later published in The Listeners *in 1912, was also admired by Ralph Hodgson.*
The youngest monkey in de la Mare's The Three Mulla-Mulgars, Nod, *"is a nizza-neela, or one who has magic in him." Thomas is referring to de la Mare's youngest child, Colin.*

Wick Green
Petersfield.
28 October 1910

My dear de la Mare,
    Garnett lent me the solitary rough copy (unillustrated) of the

Mulgars for a day or two, as I have to do my Bookman article by Nov. 1. I began the book yesterday & read it greedily through — I have just finished it. I don't know how to describe my enjoyment. It is beautiful & enchanting all through, & the harmony of the whole makes many & many of the little things wonderful which would have been beautiful even if standing alone. I am too tired to do more than go through the book telling you the passages I particularly liked & they are so many that it would tire you. All the poems are very good, by the way. It is your best prose by a long way & your best book altogether. If it were not so entirely out of the reach of my powers and even of my ambitions I should be envious, & I am envious of the satisfaction which you ought to have at having written this book.

Could you possibly send me by return — not later than Sunday – a copy of the 'Three Cherry Trees' to use if necessary in my article? By the way, as the 'English Review' has not sent a proof, I suppose they are not printing my article this month. I ought not to have told you till it was out.

Please give our love & congratulations to your wife & Florence & Dick & Jenny & the Nizza-neela.

Yours ever
Edward Thomas.

83

The poet and antique-dealer Vivian Locke Ellis.

[postmarked NO 2 10]

Thank you for your letter & the Cherry Trees. I am so glad you follow how I liked the Mulgars — I was afraid I put it stupidly. The 'Morning Post' had a good notice of 'The Return' on Monday, did you see?

May I come to you next Tuesday night? But please come to St George's (if not the Villa Villa before) at 3.30 as V.L. Ellis promises to come.   E T.

84

from E.T. 11 November 1910

Don't forget to try for Maeterlinck's 'Le Princesse Maleine' trans-
lated by Gerard Harry when you are at the Library next. I hope
you will be at the Hootons' next week-end. I shall go to the Square
I think. – By the way can you get any of these French books? —
'Ecrivains Belges d'aujourdhui' by D. Horrent
'Impressions de Theâtre' vol. viii – Jules Lemaître
'L'Anarchie Littéraire' by Christophe Recolin
'Precurseurs et Revoltes' by Edmond Schuré.

85

[postmarked NO 16 10]
Will you be at St George's on Tuesday at 3.30 – 4? I am going to
the Square afterwards. I hope you will be at the Hootons on
Saturday & Sunday.   E.T.

86

De la Mare describes Feminine Influence on the Poets *in the 1 December
1910* Times Literary Supplement *as "a kind of delightful labyrinth" and it
is Thomas's "subtle inferences, flashes of enthusiasm and his literary criticism
that make his study so interesting and original."*
Thomas's review of Songs of Childhood *and* Poems *appears in the December
1910* English Review. *He writes that de la Mare "remains an entirely hidden
magician behind his work", his poems are "the purest lyrics"and "Nowhere is
the triumph of his hushed magic more complete than in the poems of childhood."*

[postmarked DE 2 10]

Your 'Times' review is very kind. It is the <u>second</u> I have had, so far
as I know.
Don't bother about 'Princess Maleine': I have bought a copy.
We suffer from continuous mists here & almost continuous cold
rain — not to speak of cold reviewing. But we are all well & hope
you are.   E T.

I should like to see the 'Westminster'   Wick Green
review if it is out.   2 December 1910
P.S. I have just seen the article on you in the 'English Review' so
mutilated & misprinted as to be infuriating.

87

In Thomas's 14 December 1910 Daily Chronicle *review, 'Pages of
Wonderland: Mulla-Mulgars and Some Other Fairy Folk' he calls de la
Mare's book "a happy and perfect inspiration, unlike anything in the past" and
"a beautiful work of art".*

.   WICK GREEN,
                                                      PETERSFIELD.
                                                      14 December 1910

My dear de la Mare,

I am very glad to get so cheerful seeming a letter after your
recent sufferings. I hope you have forgiven me for any futilities
that were not part of the trade. As usual I did my best in a hurry
which could make a motto for my Maeterlinck, by the way. It is
simply physical strength. I do nothing all day in the rain from to
10am to 1a.m. but write away about the fellow. Everything that
goes down has to stay & all afterthoughts are afterwritten. What a
trade. What I dread is getting to like it. It will never be easy,
though, so that my 'conscience' can never take a sleeping draught.
Apparently it will take less than 5 weeks. Why waste time over a
thing I could not do well if I lived till my beard touched the
ground? Instead of simulating the aggrieved Meister please send
me tips for a book on Maeterlinck either serious or comic, if that
is not too fine a distinction.

Are you going to the Square Club? Anyhow I hope you will be
at St George's on Tuesday next. I shall. Are you all well? We send
our love to you. We are well but do not like this rain. The last week
has been the worst we ever knew I think.

When will you come down? Quite early in January, when I have
got rid of the book. Promise.

      Yours ever
            Edward Thomas.

88

This letter is accompanied by an envelope with the postmark 'DE 26 10'.
Hilaire Belloc, a respected and prolific writer and historian.

WICK GREEN,
PETERSFIELD.
20 December

My dear de la Mare,

Your poem is very good & we all liked it, including Davies. You ought to have been here or we ought to have been there; still we did our best yesterday, got a bit stuffy, but not so bad. Mervyn goes to town on Wednesday & would like to come to you on Saturday afternoon to stay till Tuesday or Wednesday. I shall suggest to my mother that she puts Mervyn in a train leaving Wandsworth Common about 2.30 for Crystal Palace, & perhaps you would meet him there? My mother will probably write to you. In case of need her address is

13 Rusham Rd
     Balham S W.

I am going to get about for the next 3 days, to see Belloc at Shipley & Hodgson at Bookham, but in spirit I shall be with Maeterlinck all the time curse him. I am in a whirl now & am going to steal 3 hours this morning to work. The children will thank you for their sweets that came this morning. They & we all send our love to you all & hope you are well & lively.

Yours ever
Edward Thomas.

Section II
1911-1913 Two Writers

By 1911 de la Mare was beginning to enjoy success as a critic and reviewer. He began work as publisher's reader for Heinemann, and also started to review for the *Saturday Westminster Gazette*. D.H. Lawrence numbered among the writers he worked with, and he reviewed Thomas's *Feminine Influence on the Poets*. His poetry collection, *The Listeners*, came out in 1912 to much acclaim and he gained much support both from friends and awards for his writing, including a lifelong subscription to the London Library which he shared with Thomas. Meanwhile, Thomas was beginning to struggle financially and looked to de la Mare for help with reviewing work. Their literary relationship underwent a major shift. Thomas at times felt bitter although he continued to support de la Mare as critic, poet and friend, encouraging him through low periods. Thomas also started to experiment in fiction and autobiography, and, possibly inspired by de la Mare's writing for children and use of illustration, worked on his own retold proverbs for children, *Four-and-Twenty Blackbirds*.

89

L.L. is the London Library.
"O Royal Traveller" is a quotation from The Three Mulla-Mulgars. *On 16 January 1911 Thomas writes to Bottomley that "De la Mare's <u>Mulla Mulgars</u> was a wonderful book that grew out of a story told to his children. He is doing many good poems."*

<u>Thu</u>rsday
[postmarked JA 12 11]

I am going to be up tomorrow & probably not next week. Can you come to St Georges at 4 or so? Do if you can. I returned your books by the way to the L.L. I am just finishing the Maeterlinck &

going to stay a couple of days with Hooton. When are you coming here? N.B. I mean this as a question to be answered, O Royal Traveller. How are you & all of you? We are all very well.   E.T.

90

R.A. Scott-James wrote a mixed review of Thomas's Feminine Influence *in the 3 January 1911* Daily News: *"He has obviously found the size of his subject a difficulty" but he "has read widely and well".*

21 January 1911.

Let me know when you & Florence will come. If it is fine you will walk up, won't you? Bags & c left at the Cloak room before 5.20 will be brought up here by 7, if we tell the carter here. It ought to be fine. It is & has been horrible. Have you the Daily News review of me, by the way?   E.T.

91

Thomas is researching for The Icknield Way.

Don't forget The Dynasts please.   3 February 1911
Many thanks for your list. May I have any of these in this order?

Donne -	Old Roads etc.	1852
Kahn	Esthétique de la Rue	1901.
Howard	Roads of England & Wales	1883.
Congleton	Treatise	1838.

We missed you on Tuesday. Don't stay away again, & don't forget to think about letting Florence & Dick come at Easter.   E.T.

92

This letter encloses references to nineteenth century issues of the Spectator, *focussing particularly on the aims and ambitions of the newspaper. A pencilled note, perhaps by de la Mare, on the back of the covering letter refers to the July 6 182[3?]8, Feb 1858, May 1 and June 1861* Spectator. *Thomas was assisting de la Mare in research for his first leading article for the* Times Literary

Supplement *since August 1909. The article, occasioned by the* Spectator's *centenary, appeared on 2 March 11 as 'The Spectator': March 1, 1711'. It does not quote any of the following passages.*
De la Mare later wrote a poem, 'There once was an old, old woman', alluding to this article. It is published in the 13 September 1913 New Statesman. *Thomas admires this poem in his 4 January 1914 letter. The text of the poem is included in the note to this 1914 letter.*

[in pencil, Feb. 1911]

My dear de la Mare,
    On these 3 sheets you will find all I could collect. Whether I got the dates wrong or not, I don't know, but you will see that only 2 numbers containd [sic] anything especially interesting. Note that first number was on July 5 not 6.
            In a hurry
                Yours ever
                    Edward Thomas.

1)

Saturday July 5   1828

No. 1
[in pencil, 1911]

16pp.
beginning on outside w News of the week resembling today's Spec. very closely

price 9d

Opening paragraph:
'The principal object of a newspaper is to convey intelligence. It is proposed in the Spectator to give this, the first & most prominent place, to a report of the leading occurrences of the week. In this department, the reader may always expect a summary account of every public proceeding, or transaction of interest, whether the scene may lie at home or abroad, that has taken place within the seven days proceeding the termination of my labours; which, we wish it to be remembered, close on Saturday at midnight.'

No reference to old Spectator

2)

Spec. Feb. 6. 1858 has a
~~Literary~~ Supplement of reviews.
Feb. 27 review Trelawny 's
'Last days of Shelley & Byron'

May 1, 1858
Long article on Rentoul

'His ambition to produce a perfect paper.... He had naturally a propensity to examine every question from all points of view. He was anxious to free his mind from all prepossessions that might obscure the truth. The fusion or confusion of practices, at the time the Spectator was started, predisposed the general public to support a ~~condition~~ journal conducted in this unpartisan spirit. The coalition of Whigs & Tories had effaced the dividing line of parties....

Measures
3)

Measures more than men were the prevalent subjects of discussion; & liberal commentators & practical reformers were alike disposed to entertain measures by which administrative government might be improved. The Spectator preferred to be a "family newspaper", to record every event of social or political importance, to devote particular attention to literature, popular science, & the fine arts, & to be independent of all party connexions, etc.

Emancipation of Catholics 'first question of moment that occurred' This 'met with approbation of every candid & dispassionate mind.'

June 1861   no change of appearance or of any kind that I can detect in any of the 5 numbers for this month.

93

Together with Edward Garnett, Thomas is collecting signatures for an eventually successful petition for the award of a Civil List Pension to W.H. Davies. He

is working on several books, The Icknield Way, Lafcadio Hearn *and* Celtic
Stories. *He is also writing* The Isle of Wight *at this time.*
De la Mare had just become a publisher's reader for Heinemann.

WICK GREEN,
PETERSFIELD.
21 February 1911

My dear de la Mare,
Many thanks. We are going ahead & really hopeful unless it is
too late for this year. Newbolt has not yet replied. I hope he will
because if interested he might be powerful.

I am afraid I can't come next Tuesday. I shall only be up for the
day on <u>Wednesday</u> the 1st of March. Work is pressing & I am not
well enough to stand the evenings in town. Sounds funny but is
true. Can you get me Professor Haverfield's '<u>Romanization of
Britain</u>' & 'Who were the Romans'? Also J.G. Campbell's '<u>The
Fians</u>' with introduction by Alfred Nutt (1891) and H. d'Arbois de
Jubainville's '<u>L'Epopée Celtique en Irlande</u>' (Vol. 5 of the Cours de
Litérature Celtique. 1892) and Alfred Nutts 'Waifs & Strays of
Celtic Tradition' (1891).
I should [sic] the three underlined best of all.

I hope you are all well. We are all except one. I have had about
10 days exceptional weakness which I can't account for except by
original & more recent sin By the way, I got Maeterlinck's Consent
after all.

Are you doing Hazlitt?

Yours ever
Edward Thomas

94

By March 1911 Garnett had invited de la Mare to join his weekly Soho liter-
ary lunches, frequented by Thomas, Norman Douglas, John Masefield, Hilaire
Belloc, Muirhead Bone, W.H. Davies, W.H. Hudson, Thomas Seccombe, R.A.
Scott-James, Stephen Reynolds, occasionally Joseph Conrad and John
Galsworthy, and, later, J.D. Beresford.

I saw Hodgson. He is very busy but wants to see you at Effingham
House, Arundel St.

WICK GREEN,
PETERSFIELD.
2 March 1911

My dear de la Mare,

Thanks for the book. May I have vols. 2 & 3 of the same series
'Folk & Hero Tales' edited by D. MacInnes with notes & c by
Alfred Nutt. The Series is 'Waifs & Strays of Celtic Tradition. Also
Emile Souvestre's 'Foyer Breton' or 'Derniers Bretons' or some
collection of Breton tales (if possible of the heroic sort) by
Villemarqué or another. I shall be grateful for any of these.

I could have come on Tuesday after all. Rushed up to town that
evening in order to spend a full day at the Museum & then found
it shut for 4 days. To make things worse I had a return of fearful
weakness & it is still with me. I am told it is only a step in my
progress towards being a new man (by vegetarianism & 2 meals a
day). I hope so. But it makes me helpless. I shall be up on
Wednesday week (15th), I am not sure about this Tuesday but
probably I shall be up, & at St George's. I am so pressed with work
– very little reviewing though – that I feel as if I ought to shut
myself up for a year. Don't want to a bit, but when I am such a
wreck I can't help it.

I hope you are all well.

The petition went in yesterday. Lloyd George, Grey, Burns &
Lord Pentland are likely to favour us. Curious but the only refusals
or silences were from Yeats, Binyon, Newbolt, Masefield, Bridges.
I enclose Masefield's letter — I lent him 'Nature Poems'. It will
amuse you: please burn it.

> With our love
> Yours ever
> ET.

[Enclosed letter:]

30, MAIDA HILL WEST,
W.
1 March, 1911.

Dear Mr Thomas,

I am sorry: but with a very special press of work & anxiety I
could not read enough of Mr Davies' work to enable to me sign

your petition as it stands. I am tempted to sign it on the grounds that the virtue which can remain attached to beautiful things, after years of hard-ship, deserves to be rewarded; but that would hardly be fair to Mr Davies, nor quite what you yourself want.

Thank you for lending me this book; it was very kind of you. I am sorry that I do not know more of Mr Davies' writing.

With kind regards
Yours sincerely
John Masefield.

95

Arthur Ransome, whom Thomas knew well, wrote a full-length Bookman *feature on Thomas, celebrating his achievements as critic and country essayist. Ransome's critical study of Edgar Allan Poe was reviewed by de la Mare in the 4 March 1911* Saturday Review. *De la Mare mainly makes use of the article to give his own critique of Poe, in which, in a paraphrase of Shelley's* Defence of Poetry, *he argues for the primacy of the "impulse or inspiration", to be followed by "tedious, conscious and critical clarification and refinement".*

WICK GREEN,
PETERSFIELD.
6 March 1911.

My dear de la Mare,

I am afraid you thought I was coming this week. But it's next week. Will you be at St George's on Tuesday for tea? Also in any case may I come to you to supper on Wednesday & remain a vegetarian? I have been better & am not. Still I shall stick to it.

By the way we got Bridges to read & digest Davies, to approve & to sign.

Your 'Saturday' review of Ransome is very good.

Now I do hope I shall see you next Tuesday and Wednesday.

Yours ever
ET.

96

Nizza Neel is a reference to The Three Mulla-Mulgars *and the rhyme itself is a tribute to de la Mare's verse.*

6 March 1911

Thank you for promising books.

I can manage Wednesday <u>next week</u> & hope that is what you mean. I have written to Henry promising. Tell me if you will be up on the Tuesday, because if so I will be at St George's, otherwise probably not. Thank you for your letter. I am feeling better – as you can guess by the Nizza Neel rhyme.

E.T.

97

Written in purple pencil. The reference to "3 books in hand" in this undated letter suggests early 1911, particularly since Thomas also uses this phrase in a 23 February 1911 letter to Bottomley of The Icknield Way, Lafcadio Hearn *and* Celtic Stories.

Satu<u>rd</u>ay

My dear de la Mare,

Thanks. I will come on <u>Tuesday</u> to the Temple Café at 4 unless I hear from you against it (I shall be at Hooton's on Monday night). You don't mention time or day but I take it you meant precisely instead of what I suggested at St George's. I am sorry you feel a bit tired, but hope you have work at any rate. I have my 3 books in hand but too little reviewing. Still feeling poorish yet am at this moment s<u>tart</u>ing to walk from Brighton home, but shall probably get a lift in a train before long – I wouldn't have started but it is an annual arrangement with Lupton. O I forgot to say that I would like to come back with you on Tuesday.

I will try to bring back one of your books.

With our love to you all

Yours ever

E T.

98

WICK GREEN,
PETERSFIELD.
[postmarked MR 23 11]

Can you renew a good custom & turn up at St George's at 4 next Tuesday? If you could be at the London library at 3 30 I would return your books. Send me a card. I hope you are much better than you were last week.

ET.

99

Thomas's introduction to Isaac Taylor's Words and places: illustrations of history, enthnology and geography *states that it is better to use "pure imagination than rash science in handling place names". This reflects his high estimation of place names as vivid poetic explorations of place and sources of creativity. Thomas makes creative use of place name lists in his work, particularly in* The South Country *and in his 1916 poems to his children. Such use of lists was common at the time. De la Mare explores lists of plant names, as in 'The Hawthorn hath a deathly smell', published in* The Listeners, *1912, and mentioned in Thomas's* Bookman *review of this collection. See also de la Mare's 'A Widow's Weeds',* Peacock Pie, *1913. Thomas anthologises both poems in* Flowers I Love, *1916.*
This letter shows Thomas sharing de la Mare's fascination with dreams and use of them as creative inspiration.

WICK GREEN,
PETERSFIELD.
29 March 1911

My dear de la Mare,

    Can you lend me those essays by members of the British Association including Bradley on place names? I had a strange dream last night. It began with me crouching with a great fear of something I could not see but which I knew to be dragonish behind me & just about to grip me by the nape of the neck. Then someone I knew but could not see – & I don't know who – bent down & whispered in a terrific voice: '<u>He</u> is in the orchard'. Then he bent nearer & whispered still lower & more terrific: 'There <u>is</u> no orchard.'* This is my copyright. Don't forget to work in a visit here

for Dick in the Easter holidays — after Easter itself would be best.
My wife & I send our love to you all.
Yours ever
ET.
Is my dream water, love, or what?

*This was so alarming in its significance that I awoke.

100

The influential writer, Edith Sichel.

P.S. Would you send a line
to Henry?
I forget his   WICK GREEN.
address.   PETERSFIELD.
[postmarked AP 8 11]

Can you be at St George's at 4 on Tuesday? If you see Miss Sichel
you might remind her to return Davies' 'Farewell to Poetry' to me.
I hope you all bear up against the winter.
ET.

101

WICK GREEN,
PETERSFIELD.
12 April 1911

My dear de la Mare,
Can Dick come on Friday the 21st. Then I will bring him up
with me on the Tuesday. Of course he can have a week end ticket
for that time. In the evening we might go to Henry's. Let me know
soon if you will come with me, so that I can write to him. And what
is his address? It is a lovely day & I am sorry Dick can't be here at
once. But we are packed full for the week end. If, however, any day
soon after Easter Monday would suit you better it will suit us
equally well.
With our love to you all
Yours ever
Edward Thomas.

We are very glad you are coming to Harting again: come to Goodwood.

102

Thomas was researching his critical biography of Lafcadio Hearn.

WICK GREEN,
PETERSFIELD.
18 April 1911

My dear de la Mare,
Can you lend me Hearn's
'Stray leaves from Strange Literatures'
'Two Years in French West Indies'
'Exotics & Retrospectives'
'A Japanese Miscellany'
and George M. Gould's 'Concerning Lafcadio Hearn'?' I am going to town this evening & could meet you any day this week to get the books. Let me know at
13 Rusham Rd
Balham   SW.
Ŀ
If you can't come to Henry's next Tuesday could you manage Monday? I am leaving it to you to arrange for both of us as you have his address. I am very sorry I shall not be here with Dick but if he know[s] my present condition he will not share my sorrow.
Yours ever
Edward Thomas.

103

Thomas's bouts of depression and ill-humour lead him to work away from home, here at his parents' house.

13 Rusham Rd
Balham SW.
20 April 1911

My dear de la Mare
Thanks for your note. I suppose mine to you got astray. It was

enclosed in one of my wife's to yours, & informed you that I was here & hereabouts for a few days. As you will be sending Dick off tomorrow – very likely by the 3.45 — can't we meet at the station & then go & have tea? Let me know this, & let my wife know the train to meet. But in case tomorrow's tea is inconvenient to you we will meet on Tuesday. I should very much like to come home with you & think I will if you don't decide against me on such an occasion. — I am here working & for the purpose of saving my family from myself.

Yours ever
ET.

104

De la Mare rarely wrote on place names. Thomas was fascinated by them.
Thomas is travelling, researching for The Icknield Way.
The "various books" include The Icknield Way, George Borrow, *and* Lafcadio Hearn. *He also spent the summer planning studies of Pater and Swinburne.*
Davies's new wooden leg was sponsored by Thomas and various friends.

WICK GREEN,
PETERSFIELD.
16 May 1911

My dear de la Mare,

I couldn't write that long letter after all. I walked & noted hard all day & in the evenings never read or wrote a line except what was compulsory. Nor did my rambling thoughts light upon a subject for a book for you. But please write a poem on 'Puck Shipton' the name of an old farm close to the road I was following. The poem will enliven my dreary page. I had fine walking weather & good country but didn't get much that was new about my road. I got quite off the track & lost a whole day. Do you remember any references to drovers & their routes with cattle? These might help me a lot. I heard of some from farmers but could not really understand more than scraps, & they were seldom explicit. A man would say: 'You could take sheep from here to Marlborough and not touch water — no, I'm telling an untruth. You would have to cross the Wylye' (which rises only a mile from where we sat). But somehow beyond waving his arm to show the first ridge he never made the road clear. I saw oxen ploughing in one place. The apple blossom in Somerset was nearly at its best. I think I have made out the Winterbourne Stoke of Hudson's 'Shepherd's Life'. I am only just back and have much work & all difficult. I want some easy reviewing to start on after so much exercise. Will you be at St George's next Tuesday at 4 or at the London Library at 3.30? I shall return a book & should like another. Can you let me have any of those I asked for and also one of Charles G. Harper's books on English roads — the Exeter road or any other road going to Devon or Cornwall. If he has a book on the old coach roads I should like to see that. When are you coming down? In a couple of months you will be at Harting, but come here before if you can. I may be overwhelmed by my various books later on. The children are back at school & as glad as we are. I hope you are all well. With our love

       Yours ever
         Edward Thomas.

P.S. Have you the volumes of Davies I lent Miss Sichel? Davies is home again: found his leg wouldn't stand steady walking — it is a costly leg more for ostentation than use.

Have you got my 'Light & Twilight'?

105

Hearn worked for some time as correspondent for Harper's Weekly *in Martinique, and the full title of* Youma, *published in 1890, reads* Youma: the story of a West-Indian slave.
Thomas cultivates de la Mare as a walking companion during his practical research.
Farewell to Poesy *and* Nature Poems *are both by W.H. Davies.*
De la Mare had been considering writing a second book on the Mulla-Mulgars.

              WICK GREEN,
              PETERSFIELD.
              28 May 1911

My dear de la Mare,
   If you are going into town soon after you get this could you have

any of these books sent to me?

Hearn's   '2 Years in the French West Indies'
                 'Stray Leaves from Strange Literatures'
                 'Youma'.

I have all the others, & by the way I don't want Harper's 'Exeter Road' but if you can get C. Deeming's 'Byways' I should like to see it I will bring back all these books on Tuesday week, & should be very glad to have them & get them read & done with at once. I still have 2 books from the L.L. & will bring them back.

Don't give up the idea of continuing the 'Mulgars'; at least don't crush the slightest impulse to do it, as I am sure nearly everybody but yourself will be very glad if it is done.

I am probably going to do the East Anglian & Chiltern part of my road next week. Could you share any part of it? You couldn't refuse it in this weather but I can't get away at the moment. The solitary objection I can suggest is that for economy's sake I shall have to cover as much ground as possible each day, & perhaps you would not like that. With our love to all of you

Yours ever
E T.

If you write slip my 'Farewell to Poesy' inside your letter, please — or is it 'Nature Poems'?

I will bring up the books with me & take them to the Library on Tuesday week & meet you there or at St George's a little later.

106

Drouth, another word for drought.

WICK GREEN,
PETERSFIELD.
14 June 1911

My dear de la Mare,

You were lucky not to come. I did 150 miles in my six days & half of it in a hard hot grit – it had to be done & looking back I have discovered some pleasures. I got home last night & there was a book from you and the London Library. Many thanks. I wish I had seen you in town but I left early on Tuesday & saw no one. Probably I shall only be up for a few hours next week on Wednesday. Can you be at St George's early that day? I wish you would come back with Hodgson & me that evening. Do. There is to be a bonfire on the high field just west of us. Do come. In any case let me know. I shall bring a copy of 'Light & Twilight' for you. Being hard up I delayed sending you one in the hope you might get it as a reviewer. I hope you are all well now. My wife & Myvanwy are in town. Here we are well but eager for rain. The drouth silences the birds & I want a change. Your letter did not reach me, by the way, until I was some distance on my road. With love to you all.

   Yours ever
   E T.

107

WICK GREEN,
PETERSFIELD.
[postmarked JU 19 11 and then JU 20 11 from Anerley]

I really will bring back your books on Wednesday & take them to the L.L. at 3.30 hoping to see you there but otherwise leaving them in your name. I will try to remember your 'John Lyly' too.

   E.T.

108

Netherhampton was the home of Henry Newbolt. On de la Mare's visits there he mixed relaxation with work, spending much of the day with Newbolt, working in his study.

WICK GREEN,
PETERSFIELD.
25 June 1911

My dear de la Mare,
 It is your right to complain now. But I have my Lafcadio Hearn

& Icknield Way both in dread & immediate proximity — Hodgson has been here 4 days & I am going to set upon the Hearn as soon as he leaves. So what can I write, especially about Thackeray? Have you discovered why he was called Makepeace? Was he a great as well as a tall & stout man? I read a book by him once of which I remember & shall never forget the title – 'Esmond.'

Congratulations on your tennis and bowls. I wish it had been at Wick Green instead of Netherhampton. But here our only sport is eating strawberries. We are naturally jealous of invaders, but will have you without any condition whatever. When do you get to Harting? If only I can get rid of Hearn by then & get under way with Icknield Street we will make August 'one grand sweet song'. I shall be up on Wednesday week, -- for the afternoon only, so far as I can see. Can you be at St George's at 4 or not later? I returned your books last Wednesday – don't want any more at present. But by the way I do want my copy of W.H.D's 'Farewell to Poesy'. I hope you are all well. My love to you.

> Yours ever
> ET.

109

De la Mare had been writing reviews for the Saturday Westminister Gazette *for some time. He met its literary editor, Naomi Royde-Smith, in the spring of 1911. They quickly became very close indeed.*
With the arrival of his third child and consequent temporary loss of his wife's small earnings, a drop in reviewing, and his expensive house on the hangers of Steep, Thomas is struggling to cope financially.

> Tuesday
> [in pencil July 1911]

My dear de la Mare,

I didn't want to bother about it this afternoon but I have been thinking you might feel able to speak to Miss Royde Smith in such a way that she would give a chance to any articles I send to the Westminster. I don't want you to think of doing anything that might seem awkward or likely to be ineffective or in any way to put you in a difficult position. Only if you think it might help please do what may occur to you. I have very little work & things are not hopeful. We have been thinking it may be necessary to move to a cheaper house & school, but cannot decide until we are compelled, which I hope we shan't be. Please do not think it has ever occurred to me, by the way, that I should <u>review</u> for the Westminster. That I could not do unless I knew for certain that it would not affect you & it certainly would. I know it might enter your mind to suggest reviewing, but I do not want you to consider it for a moment or to mention the question if you write to me.

       Yours ever
       Edward Thomas

110

"American" could refer to Fry's Magazine, *which published, with illustrations, two of Thomas's poetic essays: 'In the Crowd at Goodwood' in July 1911 and 'Chalk Pits, the "Travellers' Rests" of the people of the Road' in October 1911. On the righthand edge of this letter, to be read vertically from bottom to top, is the watermark 'WATERTON', the lowest letter of which, 'W', starts just above Thomas's reference to his high water mark.*

                   WICK GREEN,
                   PETERSFIELD.
                   10 July 1911

My dear de la Mare,

    Thank you. I shall now look for something as cheerful as possible & send it to the Westminster unless I hear that it will be safer to send it via Miss Royde Smith. I am trying various possibilities including an American. I hope your American publisher will do something sensible & immediate. My difficulty is chiefly due to having to write books which are costly & pay less than reviews. I have spent a quarter of the amount to be paid for my Icknield Way in travelling & books already. Only a direct & efficient interference from Providence can really improve things. I have got to my high water mark. You pretty certainly have not & I know most people would agree with me in saying this.

    I don't know when I shall be up again & perhaps not for 3 weeks. But I will let you know & also tell you the Goodwood days. At present I don't need any books, by the way: thank you. I hope Dick will get very well & the others not get ill & then with the help of this kind of weather we will get some fun out of August.

       Yours ever
       ET.

111

WICK GREEN,
PETERSFIELD.
18 July 1911

My dear de la Mare,

I expect to be in town next week. Can you be at St George's on Tuesday? Come as early as you can. I haven't yet learnt the date of Goodwood but hope it is the week after you come. We are looking forward to your coming. It is possible I shall have my Icknield Way book well begun by then & I shall be not too busy & not too troubled by the thing. I am going to bring back your Lyly if I can think of it on Tuesday.

Yours ever
Edward Thomas.

112

"Mullabuls", a playful reference to The Three Mulla-Mulgars.
An illustrated version of Thomas's 'In the Crowd at Goodwood' was published in the July 1911 issue of Fry's Magazine.
Florence is probably at Thomas's house.
Both Hodgson and Naomi Royde-Smith visited while the de la Mares were at Harting this summer.

WICK GREEN,
PETERSFIELD.
19 July 1911

My dear de la Mare of Mullabuls,

Thank you about the Westminster, but I am sorry – and so will everybody else be — to hear your news. I hope you will get thro it with the least possible trouble & not fail to keep your appointment at Harting. If you should be in doubt or delayed could you possibly come down here for a few days & fit in Goodwood? No I expect not, but if you can I hope you will. I shall see you on Tuesday in bed or out of bed & please tell me what you have thought about Light & Twilight. Is the short 'article' of 1200 — 2000 words to be avoided (except for a living)? Must I burn my old notebooks as well as refuse to keep new ones? I have begun my Icknield way & what about your American? You don't say. What do you do besides your 'Times' & 'Westminster' work? I hope stories & poems at not too long or increasing intervals. I have written nothing this year but what I had to — so much reading & wayfaring have I had.

      With our love to all of you except of course Florence.

      Yours ever
        ET.

P.S. As they have not issued any notice of it at the station yet I suppose Goodwood is not next week but the week after & I hope Hodgson may come down for it.

113

Thomas is in Wales, finishing The Icknield Way. *This note is written in pencil.*

      Llandilo
      Caermarthenshire
      Tuesday
      [postmarked 12 SEP 11]

Can you be at St George's to tea on Thursday? Or if you are in town come to Miles' to lunch.

      ET.

P.S. Can you bring back that old book of Receipts that I lent you?

114

Both de la Mare and Thomas wrote epitaphs. Thomas anthologised them in A Pocket Book, *included an essay called 'Epitaphs as a Form of English Literature' in his 1902* Horae Solitariae, *and praised de la Mare's 'An Epitaph' in his 4 November 1908 letter. De la Mare published this poem in* The Listeners, *1912, and Thomas quotes it in his* In Pursuit of Spring, *1914, and anthologises it in* This England, *1915, echoes of it also surfacing in his own poem, 'The Unknown', composed on 14 February 1916.*
Thomas is suffering from weakness and depression.
On 16 September, Thomas asks Edward Garnett for suggestions for "an article or series connected with a voyage, say on a Welsh trading ship to the Mediterranean ports, perhaps as far as Constantinople", and on 20 September

suggests that the English Review *"might take something"*.

[in pencil, Sept 1911]

My dear de la Mare,

 I was sorry not to see you. So was Hodgson. But come next week on Tuesday — I shall almost certainly be up then & will let you know if I am not. I can't promise to come to supper as my people are away & where I stay I ought to sup. No I don't feel better. Things are all so troublesome & then there is myself. I don't know how it will settle. I am chucking my 2 meal theology in spite of today's 'Chronicle'. How is your work & when are the poems coming? Please remind your wife she was to send me a magazine article containing some of your epitaphs. Can you get me a job which would mean a month at sea? Give my love to them all.

   Yours ever

    ET

P.S. I have just had a note from Ellis. He & his wife are just getting a house near East Grinstead & they want Hodgson to procure a mildly dangerous dog for them. He says he will come to St George's on Tuesday, when the first picnic of a new (but 17th century) house is over.

115

De la Mare's suggestions relate to Thomas's Lafcadio Hearn.
Hearn wrote Kwaidan *in 1904.*

     Wick Green
     Friday
     [in pencil, Sept 22 1911]

My dear de la Mare,

 I have used all your suggestions & was very glad of them. 'The number of stories increases: 'Kwaidan' contains little else' — is altered to 'the stories increase in number'. Is that right, sir? How fond your heart must be of your boots to go on such provocation. I am sorry to hear it. Hadn't you better come to sea to get it up again? I expect I shall not be away much above a month, but nothing is arranged yet. Could you, by the way, lend me Gissing's book on Sicily, and the 'Brut y Tywysogion' (=roughly Brit er Towisogion) in the 'Rolls' series?

I will be at St George's at 3.30 on Tuesday if I don't go to the London Library steps at 3.15 or earlier.

      With our love
        Yours ever
          ET.

116

Thomas had done some research for a book on Borrow with Methuen in 1907 and 1908. The book eventually appeared in 1912 with Chapman and Hall. This letter has the penciled date of 27 October 1911, and, deleted, the years 1909 and 1910-1914. The letter appears to bring news of the renewed Borrow project and a 23 October 1911 letter refers to this as a project de la Mare already knows about. On 4th October 1911 Thomas informs Garnett of the likelihood that the sea voyage will not take place due to lack of work and worries about peace of mind although 'I had already been offered a choice of Cardiff ships to the Black Sea or Port Said.'
The 'Royal Traveller' comes from The Three Mulla-Mulgars.

               Wick Green
               Friday
               [Early October 1911]

My dear & Royal Traveller,

    After all I am not going away, at least not by sea. I am going to do a book on Borrow instead. So can you lend me these books for quite a short time as I am going to work furiously? –

    Captain Alexander Smith's 'Highway[-]men' 1720.

    C.G. Leland's 'Gypsies'.

    Richard Head & Francis Kirkman's 'English Rogue'.

    Hindes-Groome's 'In Gypsy Tents' and also his edition of (I think) 'Lavengro'

I hope you will be at St George's on Tuesday early if not at the Mt Blanc before. If I don't hear from you or see you at lunch I will come to the Library at 3 & bring back the <u>Brut</u> I borrowed.

    I hope you didn't mind my feeble little note with your poems, but I was so pressed with a lot of little things & I didn't want to keep you waiting. Are you all well?

      Yours ever   ET.

117

Museum
[in pencil 1911]

My dear de la Mare,

I am very sorry to do this. It is depression & nothing more. There is nowhere I should so much like to be as at your house now but I dare not come. I came up to town not dreaming I should not see you but the thing is too strong. After myself I am chiefly sorry for your wife as I fear I shall have warned you too late to save her trouble. Please ask her to forgive me. I expect it will pass over & let me come again if you will. I took back your L.L. books & saw the Romantic Ballads at the Museum.

Your sorry
ET.

118

In a 16 September letter to Garnett, Thomas asks for suggestions for articles to write on a sea voyage, and writes again on 4 October, apologising for any trouble because of cancelling this project. Possibly the reference to Thomas Seccombe, writer and assistant editor of the Dictionary of National Biography, *is related to this.*

13 Rusham Rd
23 October 1911

My dear de la Mare,

I am hoping you didn't think any ill of my not coming. I believe you wouldn't if you knew. Please don't write or mention the ghastly thing. It may all be past in a day or two. I am sorry I lost the evening especially as I shall have no sort of peace now till this accursed Borrow is off my mind (to use a euphemism). Don't write unless you want to say you never for a moment thought I was playing you the same trick as I did Seccombe.

Yours ever
ET.

119

*Thomas's wife, alarmed at Thomas's swinging moods, wrote to his old friend
the writer-solicitor E.S.P. Haynes, who offered to pay for Thomas to have a
holiday in Laughharne, Carmarthenshire.*

P.S. You might like to see this show

> Wick Green
> Petersfield.
> 30 October 1911

My dear de la Mare,

I was very glad to have your letter but things were not much
better for several days & since I have got back to a kind of ease I
have been very busy finishing off bits of work & c because I am
probably going away for 2 or 3 months at once. I should go to sea,
only the Borrow must be done. So I am coming up to town tomorrow (Tuesday), with no certainty as to what I shall do except that
I shall take a train into Wales on Wednesday or Thursday at latest.
I hope you are not busy or otherwise engaged on Tuesday. If you
are not I want to see you. If you are in town, could you meet me
at St Georges at 4 & let me come home with you? If you aren't I
hope I may come to you at about 7. Only, I don't know how you
can let me know. I will chance it, unless you cd get a message to
me c/o Hodgson at Fry's.

I wish you could help, but I am afraid nobody can except by
chance. The combination of things against me at present is rather
formidable but a friend of mine has offered me money which
makes this coming change easy except that it takes me away from
everyone.

> With our love
> ET.

120

Thomas is doing some preliminary reading for his book on Swinburne.
*On 12 October 1909, Thomas comments to Bottomley that "so far the best
things I have done have been about houses. I have quite a long series – I
discover, tho I did not design it." The poem he praises most in de la Mare's*

1912 The Listeners *features a house:* '*The Dwelling Place*'.

> c/o Mrs Wilkins
> Victoria St
> Llaugharne
> Caermarthenshire
> [7 or 9] November 1911

My dear de la Mare,

I only write this to show I have the will. I can't talk on paper &
I am too tired of writing ordinary printed Thomas to give you any
of it even if you are not too tired of reading it. There is nothing
wrong with this place. It is chiefly one long plain silent street with
a church above it at one end among trees & a castle at the other
end where a brook runs into a great wide estuary between two
wooded headlands & c. & c. The people are very nice so far &
especially Mrs Wilkins who is 45, stout, cooks well & daily regrets
that I don't eat at tea. I don't, except that it might hasten & enliven
the end. I am writing too much Borrow every morning & most
evenings. What else can I do as I can't do anything out of doors
except walk & can't do very much of that? I can't read – except a
page a day of the Complete Poems of Gosse. Please ask a difficult
question or two about Borrow so that I may fill some pages with
trying to answer. Also will you send me from the L.L. Elijah
Waring's Life of Edward Williams, the Bard of Glamorgan? If you
cd send it soon I shd be more than ever yr obliged servant. I wish
you wd come here for a time. You cd write at least one poem about
each house in the town. Also I shd be very glad. I have no
company except myself, & only half of him; not even a pipe. If you
do see Hodgson give him my love but I believe he does not love
me.

I am yours & Mrs de la Mares & the children's ever

E.T.

121

Thomas writes reviews for Davies's Songs of Joy *for the 30 January* Daily
Chronicle, *the February* Bookman, *and in a Christmas letter to Bottomley
records a request from Harold Monro for an unpaid review on Davies for his
new* Poetry Review. *A review of Davies appears, published in the February*

1912 edition, unsigned, but with the curious initials 'A.H.J'. Thomas prophesies this journal "will die at the 5th or 6th number unregretted except by Poets whose circulation was guaranteed by the Poetry Society to reach 1,000. A home for incurables."
Thomas reviews Lewis Melville's The Life and Letters of Laurence Sterne *in the 17 November 1911* Daily Chronicle.
De la Mare's new poems become The Listeners and Other Poems, *1912.*

c/o Mrs Wilkins
Victoria St
Llaugherne [sic]
Caermarthenshire
19 November 1911

My dear de la Mare,
    To tell you the truth I was beginning to think you a pig. But I know what it is. Either one writes at once — as I am doing — and says nothing or puts it off in the hope of better times & then finally says nothing with the same Despatch. I like hearing from you though. I feel uncommonly unreal here for days together, never uttering a word that goes with a thought except on paper. A week ago I met an old innkeeper I could get on with but he is 6 miles away & over the ferry & perhaps another day he wd repent having talked so much. As a rule I feel myself (in a less aggravated way) rather as I did a day or two back, walking into a village near Tenby as the school was coming out, & one of the boys looking at me as if I were deaf or marble said to another: 'He is exactly like a skeleton.' He was inaccurate, but the differences are mostly to my disadvantage. I envy you reviewing, I do indeed; but I don't mean I am envious of you; indeed I am not, but very glad. Sometimes I can scarcely believe my bad luck. Not a book since I came here except Davies' poems. No one sent me Borrow's letters even – not one. A year ago I really thought I shd always be at that moderate but [?] very uneasy level, & now there seems nothing for it but 7 books a year, as I shall have done when this Borrow is finished. Or perhaps more, as several of these were paid for at £1 or even 25/- a 1000 words, & my price will go down.
    I don't know why I stay here. Its sole advantage is that I don't (much) worry my wife & my children not at all. Otherwise I now know that no kind of air, food, scene, or regimen can affect me seriously. There is something wrong at the very centre which

nothing deliberate can put right, but some thing or somebody "spiritual" may put it right at any moment in some inexplicable way. Sometimes for an hour in the dark & the rain I think the something has come, but day after day I believe it can never come. If I could have work & <u>remain alone</u> to do it I think I could shut my mouth, but the two difficulties together might in a short time put any solution out of the question. I don't know if I ought to write here (with not even a forlorn hope) just because it is not my own money I am wasting. — I thought I had Waring's book from the L.L. once. It is far too rare & costly for me to buy the only & poor little volume. The only other books I should like to see are that 'Brut y Tywysogion' (ed. by Ab Ithel in the Rolls Series about 1856)

& 'Gerald the Welshman' by ~~Henry (?) [Jones?]~~. Henry Owen

I would like these, tho I don't know if I shall read them. Except Giraldus I really haven't read anything whatever since I came down. I don't want to & I even try not to when indoor boredom suggests it which is seldom.

I also want to know if 40 brings conscious relief or only another kind of need for relief from 50.

Yours ever (& Mrs de la Mare's even if she is angry with me for not agreeing with her about your Early Works)

E.T.

P S. Did you think the Sterne review from any point of view a <u>mistake</u>?

<u>One other book I want</u> is your new poems & also ample warning as to the exact date of publication.

I am afraid this letter is unanswerable. No hurry about the books.

122

The Return *wins the Royal Society of Literature's Polignac Prize of £100 for a 'promising' book in November 1911.*
Jenny, usually known as Jinny, and Colin are de la Mare's two youngest children. Thomas becomes Colin's godfather sometime this year.
Naomi Royde-Smith of the Saturday Westminister Gazette.

An unsigned 28 October 1911 Saturday Westminster Gazette *review of Thomas's* Maeterlinck *is critical but approving, calling it "a fascinating study" and writing that "we can imagine no better treatment of the plays than the half-tender almost regretful analysis to which Mr. Thomas subjects them, though in our opinion he does scant justice to the most impressive".*
Percy Lubbock's 23 November 1911 Times Literary Supplement *review of Thomas's* Maeterlinck *discusses Maeterlinck but hardly mentions Thomas.*

Saturday
[in pencil, after 24 November 1911]

My dear de la Mare

This is good news. Your wife told me to expect something good, but I cd not think what it wd be. Then I missed it in the Chronicle – how you must chuckle over the way they accept 'The Return' as the 'best piece of literature of the year' & speak of you as 'wellknown & c'. My only grumble is that the good Committee chose The Return. I have nothing against the Return. But what had they against the Mulgars except that it was not a serious work? I am sorry too that it is not annual & perpetual, & that you can't ever get it again however long you live. I hope you are all having a jollification. Or will you postpone it till I come back? But I might have only one night in town & that I shd have to spend with my people – so you had better have it now & do without the skeleton at the feast if you can, tho it is an ancient Egyptian custom. What does Jenny say – What does Colin say? I should like to know exactly.

Now as to myself have I not made much more already out of your books than you have? If they had known this they wd have given me the prize, not as a rich author but as a much cleverer one than you. Why shd I not allow you to have the advantage <u>for a time</u>? Besides I am living now in some luxury at no expense to myself. I enter a town & I do not slink about looking for a place where I can have haricots & lemonade but I enter the principal door of the 'Half Moon' & order steak & chipped potatoes & a pint of ale, & if an apple tart appears with cream I eat a good deal of that also & I pay the bill almost without thinking whether it might have been less over at the 'Crown'. So then anything from you is an additional luxury. If you still insist, I give you a choice of two, the first one rather expensive & that is a week's visit on the part of the Royal Traveller to the Borough of Llaugharne. I had been thinking before of asking you to come & put it down in the bill of my expenses which as I told you are being paid for me. Will this move you?* If not, the second choice is a Rocking chair, plain, with arms & without springs. Here my imagination & even my needs cease for the moment. On Monday I go to St Davids for 2 days [.] After that I shall be ready to receive you here. I shall at once send Miss Royde Smith an embarrassing choice of prose.

Please tell your wife I was really glad as well as relieved to hear that after all we did agree about your Bérol: also that if I possibly can I will come before Christmas & see about those apples.

Your news & a walk in a still sunny & frosty air has you see made me rather less myself than usual. I had a day in Swansea in the middle of the week, but Borrow grows very fast indeed & if you see any interesting reviews of his Letters I wish you wd send them.

As for us I can see now I shall leave here about December 18 or 19. Then I cd at least see you at tea time on that day if no more. With love to you all

     Yours ever
     ET

I   The 2 books came today & many thanks. Waring is not in the Library, they tell me.

II   I've no idea who did the Times review. It was kind & might apparently have been more so without difficulty – By the way, in my book I said that Maeterlinck not only could but would write beautifully on a broomstick. He has now proved it by sending a fairly long letter praising my book on him.

III   By the same post as yours came an invitation to subscribe to the Authors Society Pension fund

IV   May I see the Evening News interviewer's prose?

V   Will you send me a list of subjects for my next year's 7 books? Some biography & critical, some not. This is serious

VI & lastly. I positively invite questions about Borrow. Think of some now. At St George's you wd not fail, & here, as my pen is mightier than my tongue, I might be able to answer – in book form.

* We will go halves. That is a good plan.

123

Thomas's youthful passion for Pater has transmuted into impatience with decorative and deliberately thought-out language.
Borrow wrote Lavengro.
In de la Mare's The Three Mulla-Mulgars *the monkeys call leopards 'Roses'.*

Llaugharne
12 December 1911

My dear de la Mare, I had quite given you up. For each of the last fourteen days I had looked for a letter. It would not amuse you if I told you what I thought sometimes. However you are incorrigible & so you see am I, as I am writing an hour after getting yours. Pity your guesses about Borrow didn't come earlier for I have had a string of dismal days & could only write & write, so I finished the book yesterday and what is more sealed it up ready for the post. Curse it. Still it has saved me about 35 long days boredom tho it has also give[n] me a large proportion of sleepless nights. I have never slept so ill.

About Pater & French. Pater read a lot of French. The story I <u>heard</u> was that he wd not read Stevenson for fear & c. I wish he had known 30 languages & done something else to make his ridiculous millinery and icework impossible. I daresay the 30 did make the 31st (English) almost as foreign as they: you know how impersonal as far as vocabulary & rhythm his style usually is. He knew them very imperfectly by the way. I don't believe I have used the word imaginative about him once. So I daresay he is the <u>thing</u>. He admired Cobbetts character & style tho he hates his opinions – he mentions C. in Lavengro. They had resemblances. Both wrote a good deal straight after long days in the saddle. Both opinionated violent men, but Cobbett bluff & Borrow quite overbearing & a bully.

<u>Are</u> your roses <u>roses</u> or are they leopards [With?] That ambiguity apart the verses are A1 at 5 Warbeck Rd or I should say at Llaugharne. Why didn't you come? I really meant it. Much more than the chair. Still I am determined to have a chair rocking chair of the simplest armed kind with plain wood rockers. But you wouldn't buy me one, would you? I would really like it, but I meant the alternative to compel you to come yourself out of ostentation, preferring to spend £3 or so to under £1!

I sent the books back yesterday. I hardly looked at them, simply can't read at all, nothing but letters & the 2 or 3 books I was compelled to read including Borrow's Letters which are good if you don't know the Bible in Spain but small beer if you do. They are interesting though to a biographer. Thanks for offering your copy. I had to buy one. Superior devil I am. Now why didn't you send this letter before? It would have helped my book not to speak of me. As it is I did the whole thing out of a vacuum as usual. Seccombe promised help but leaves my letters unanswered. I am now frantically offering to do books on any male or female recognised by publishers. I offered Milton among others! Can you imagine. It is like offering to take a farm or to do pigsticking. Only I <u>would</u> do the Milton, but would not stick a pig.

I have some fairly good Welsh notes — I mean notes & memories I could use to fairly good purpose with time – but nobody will incite me to use them. If I go away again it may be to write a book as a speculation. Only I have got to do a book on Pater as well.

About seeing you I don't know what to do with myself here now. I was supposed to leave on Friday & come to town on Sunday. I now think to leave on Thursday. Now tell me – shall I come on you on Sunday afternoon & stay the evening? Or shall we meet in town on Monday? If so you fix time & place & please send me a word
c/o John Williams
W. WAUN WEN School
Swansea
where I shall be on Thursday. If you can't, then write to me at 13 Rusham Rd Balham on Saturday. I will do as your letter suggests. There's Christian forgiveness.
With love to you all
ET.

Monday <u>evening</u> I may be engaged.

124

Swansea.
Thursday.
[postmarked DE 15 1911]

I will come at about 4 on Sunday then, without my strait waistcoat.

But please have the chair ready. I have said all I can & leave the rest to you. It must have a back, 2 rockers & if possible arms at the sides. That is absolutely all. I leave the poetry to you.   E.T.

125

Thomas begins to develop his ideas on the relations between writing and speech, later blossoming into poetry after discussions with Frost in 1914. Jenny, de la Mare's younger daughter, usually known as Jinny.

Wick Green
31 December 1911

My dear de la Mare,

I am sorry I never wrote before especially to the children, but I hadn't a book worth sending. Did they ever get my 'Celtic Stories' that I sent from Laugharne?

Probably I shall be up next week on the 8th or 9th. Now will you – can you – fix a day when you will always be on view at St George's? I would prefer Monday which is one of your days I know. Davies would like to be sure of finding you on some certain day. Then Ellis would too & perhaps Hodgson again & I would be faithful once a fortnight or so. Could you manage it. If so I will write to Ellis & Hodgson or will you? And begin on the 8th if Monday suits. I hope your work won't worry you at first.

I am going to begin on Pater soon. Can you put me onto any books, essays or passages relating to style, especially on the connection between writing & speech? Send me any references you think of. I would like to borrow from the London Library

Thomas Wright's 'Pater'
Is it 'Thomas' though? May I have it?

Yours ever with our love to you all 5 1/2 (that is [one?] for Jenny & Colin to quarrel over)

E.T.
RSVP

126

De la Mare and Thomas exchange recommendations for research reading on style, language and prose.

Punctuation: Its Principles and Practice *offers a history of punctuation and word separation from manuscript to printed book, citing instances in medieval manuscript where the author "indicated by a dot every slight break in his thought". This is pertinent to Thomas's idiosyncratic use of spaced punctuation in his handwriting.*

The reference to an essay on English prose is not clear, although there is a review of English Prose Rhythms *in the November 1912* Bookman, *initialled D.S., and de la Mare's October 1912 contribution to the* Edinburgh Review *includes, among fourteen books, Saintsbury's* A History of English Prose Rhythm.

Wick Green
5 6 January 1912

My dear de la Mare,

I will ask Ellis to come on Monday & Hodgson & Davies may be there. Do come if you can. In any case I shall probably be there between 4 & 5. If I don't see you I will call at Heinemann's for the Pater.

Thanks for your list. De Quincey's essays on style & language I have just read. His continuity is something terrible. Raleigh I think is useless. I can't trace the essay of Newman's unless it is one on Poetry in his 'Essays Critical & Historical'. Young might be good. Can you lend him: also/or Symonds?

Suppose I don't see you on Monday, will you be visible on Tuesday at St George's? Or will you come to Eustace Miles' on <u>Monday</u> for lunch? Hodgson & I will be there. We have kissed again without tears. — I shall understand if you don't come but shall expect you. I am better.

With our love
Yours ever
ET.

By the way, if you can see T.F & M.F A Husband's 'Punctuation: its Principles & Practice' you might get a suggestion for your essay on English Prose. A Propos of what are you writing it?
See also Wordsworth's Prefaces & the Biographia Literaria, also James Milne 'Writers & Readers' twice a week in the 'Chronicle'.

127

This letter indicates de la Mare's improved financial situation, particularly as a result of the post at Heinemann.

Wick Green
Petersfield
11 January 1912

My dear de la Mare,

If you are giving up parts of your reviewing, – if you feel that you might have a voice in controlling what you give up, – if you also feel that you could recommend me, — & if you feel, furthermore, that you would be listened to while recommending me, – then would you? I don't like asking, particularly because you may want to resume the work & if I had taken it over you might not like doing so. Therefore anything I did get under these circumstances I should regard as temporary. Even so I only ask because my agent has been reminding me that there will soon be no more possible books left for me to write on commission. He bids me prepare for that winter by thinking of a novel. But that is absurd. I might write one autobiographical novel & that nobody would buy. Garnett who knows more thinks my only field is literary journalism.

I hope you don't mind my asking. It is perhaps unkind of me even to suggest you might. I do so only because the blunders of the egoist are past counting & this may be one.

Yours ever
ET.

128

Thomas considers moving to a smaller house for reasons of economy.
Martin Secker published Thomas's Swinburne *and, later, his* Pater.

13 Rusham Rd
Wednesday
[in pencil, Before March 1912]

My dear de la Mare,

I would have come tonight & had it in mind that if I heard from you I would, but yesterday Garnett asked me to call at Hampstead at 8 30 & tho I know he doesn't want to see me I must go. Between 4 & 8 to night I am free & shall be at St George's at first, and if you are in town, or can conveniently [sic] be look in. I bicycle home tomorrow. Could you come down this weekend? There won't be so many weekends now before we cease to have a spare room, as we hope to leave in March — it isn't certain.

> Yours ever
>> ET.

Swinburne is not out. I can't say why, unless Secker is improving it.

129

Henry C. Colles was already writing musical histories for schools and went on to write several more works on music, as well as editing the Groves Dictionary.
Baby is the family's pet name for Thomas's youngest daughter Myfanwy.

> WICK GREEN,
> PETERSFIELD.

My dear de la Mare,

Monday 3.15 at the L.L..

Thank you for writing. I won't write though. We have just been scared by baby: took her to the hospital yesterday for a 'very dangerous' operation, which after chloroforming was found unnecessary. She was so happy up to the nurse's coming for her. They think now that she will be all right soon. It is her stomach: she has swallowed something that does not like being there. If I shouldn't appear on Monday it will be that that keeps me, but I don't expect. It is a lovely day. When will you come down here for a change? Might I come to see you all on Tuesday if you aren't too busy to make it impossible?

> Yours ever
>> E.T.

Yes, Colles' on Composition
I am the only young — that I know in want of success.

130

WICK GREEN,
PETERSFIELD.
15 February 1912

My dear de la Mare,

Baby is much better & we hope she will be back tomorrow. What slush this Johnson is mostly.

Ever yours
ET.

131

Ferris Greenslet, editor of Atlantic Monthly *1902-1907, and then director of Houghton Mifflin Co, wrote* Walter Pater, *1911 (1903).*
This letter has the pencilled date '1914?' with 1911 deleted, but references to the loan of Greenslet, Baby's health and de la Mare's move suggest it was written in February or March 1912.
With the extra income coming in from his work with Heinemann, de la Mare moved to a quieter and more spacious house in Thornsett Road, Anerley, which allowed him to have his own room.

Wick Green.
Saturday

My dear de la Mare,

I should like to have Greenslet if you can send it soon. Probably I shan't be up for another 2 weeks or more. I was sorry not to see you. However I was good for nothing except writing (ill) about Pater, which I have just been doing & am just about to do again. Baby is quite well. I hope you will get safe & sound over the move.

Yours ever
ET.

132

On 22 March 1912 Thomas tells Bottomley that he "roughly finished a book on Pater last Sunday".

WICK GREEN,
PETERSFIELD.
[postmarked MR 17 [?]2]

If you still exist please prove it at St George's on Monday.
The author of
'Walter Pater'.
Just had your letter. I don't think I can manage Tuesday
evening, but shall be at St George's at tea time that day also. Can't
you come one day? Too late for Greenslet.

133

Tuesday
[in pencil, 19 March 1912]

My dear de la Mare,
I was very sorry indeed not to see you. Could we arrange to
lunch together on Mondays? Or have you too short an interval? I
should be glad. Probably I shall be up in a fortnight & can probably come to you, certainly will if I can. I have just been walking
from Cirencester thro Stow in the Wold & Stratford to Warwick &
Coventry. If you are in town tomorrow look in at St George's. As
I am keeping "Pater" to ripen a bit I would like <u>Greenslet</u> after all.
I have now no work except the book* & no prospects at all, but am
feeling a little better able to endure it. I shall soon envy you your
complaint of drudgery.
On the back you will see a specimen of my employer's style.
Yours and your wife's ever
ET.

* on Swinburne. Please advise or construct or undermine or
something, but don't tell anyone about it.

*[The above is written upsidedown on the back of the following letter, which
sports a* Daily Chronicle *letterhead*

THE DAILY CHRONICLE
EDITORIAL OFFICE
31 Whitefriars Street London

March 24 1912

Dear Thomas,

I am sending you tonight, not for review but for yourself a book about Chirk Castle, which, I fancy, is somewhere in the marshes of Wales in a land that always, naturally, interests you.

Yours truly,
James Milne

134

[postmarked 27 MAR 12]

I wish I could, but I have to be home tonight to do a short bit of writing in a hurry. Can you come down very soon? In any case I hope to see you on Monday the 8th or if that is a bad day then on the 10th I think I can come to Anerley.   E.T.

P.S. I forgot the 8th was Easter Monday. Then the 9th or 10th is better for me

135

Thomas is writing from the home of playwright, critic and editor Clifford Bax where the nervous disorder specialist, Godwin Baynes, who later became the champion and translator of Carl Jung, is also staying. Thomas underwent treatment with Baynes in 1912 and 1913 and probably encountered Freud's theories at this time.

Broughton Gifford
Friday.
[in pencil, c.a. 18 April 1912]

My dear de la Mare,

I am going to be in town probably all next week working at the Museum. When shall I see you? I could come almost any night and stay to breakfast — any night but Monday. Tell me also if we can meet in town. After the end of the week I am going to a farm near Orchardleigh to write my Swinburne. I am just going home after a most inspiring week of walking talking & cycling with a doctor who appears to have made me a different man though still yours ever & your wife's

Edward Thomas

Home tomorrow

PS. Can you get me a copy – not a free one unless that is very easy – of a book on Swinburne in the same series as Pater?

136

This undated letter was placed at the end of the Bodleian album but the reference to de la Mare's age helps date it: de la Mare was born on 25 April 1873.

13 Rusham Rd

My dear de la Mare,

I will gladly come & help to destroy the edifice of 38 & build up 39: I hope that as far as the outsider can see the new will not be very different from the old, except that it should include 'The Listeners.' I will come as early as I can but may not be able to by 6 as I have to see my doctor again. Alas, it was a dream, the most pleasant for many years. I don't know if it really can be perpetuated. But you know more about dreams. My love to you all.

E.T.

Look in at St George's on Thursday if possible & I might join you homeward.

137

Thomas is staying at a farm to work on his critical book on Swinburne, due to be completed by the summer.
George Saintsbury's A History of English Prose Rhythm, *published by Macmillan in 1912.*
Robert Bridges's A tract on the present state of English pronunciation, *published in book form by Oxford, Clarendon Press, in 1912.*

Dillybrook Farm, ~~WICK GREEN~~
Road, ~~PETERSFIELD~~
nr Bath.
[postmarked APR 28 12]

Has Saintsbury yet published his one-vol. abridged <u>History of Prosody</u>, & if so can you lend it to me this week: also Robert Bridges' book on metre — or is it only in a study of Paradise Lost? Please. I hope your cold is better.

E.T.

138

G.M. Trevelyan's Garibaldi and the thousand, *published by Longmans, Green in 1909.*

> Dillybrook Farm
> Road
> nr Bath.
> 2 May 1912

Could you lend me Trevelyan's two recent books 'Garibaldi & the Thousand' & the other whose name I forget?

E.T.

139

Thomas admires The Listeners. *Echoes of 'The Dwelling Place' later surface in Thomas's 'The Green Road' and 'Out in the Dark'.*
Clifford Bax admires 'Miss Loo' from the same collection.
Thomas's 24 April 1910 letter mentions Ralph Hodgson's liking for de la Mare's 'The Three Cherry Trees', which is published in The Listeners, *1912. Thomas quotes from it in his August 1912* Bookman *review and* In Pursuit of Spring, *1914, and anthologises it in* Flowers I Love, *1916.*

> Dillybrook Farm
> Road
> nr Bath
> 15 May 1912

My dear de la Mare,

Thank you. I have just looked through your book & am half glad half sorry, but more glad. Sorry to think there are so many poems in it I might have seen all these months: glad to think there are so many new ones to read. You won't suspect me of mere dull ingenious compliments when I confess I have only glanced at the book.

The fact is I am writing Swinburne & can't get free just yet so I shall leave the book to fit in this evening. You won't mind hearing that Bax admired Miss Loo (& some, that I believe you have left out, from the English Review) without being advised to. He lives 8 miles away & I spent Saturday night there. This is delicious country in the sun & now today in misty rain. There is May & nightingales at hand. I wish you could come. I can give you a bed & I believe I could manage Whitsun if you could. Tell me. Otherwise I may not be in town for another month. I am not sure. I am restless here now that I am writing. Many thanks for Saintsbury but to tell the truth I really can't read him, so I find now. The other book was G M Trevelyan's Garibaldi book or rather his 2 Italian books. If you could send them this week they would be useful, but don't trouble to send them later. When I come to town I shall be very glad to come to you if Dick doesn't mind. You aren't 40 already are you? No I wasn't too tired (for myself).

Hodgson will be pleased to see the Cherry Trees again. I am jealous of you for being able to write such unprofitable things, unprofitable even for me this time, for no one has sent it to me for review. I shall have pleasure without profit for the first time in reading you.

With my love to you all & tell me if perhaps you could come
Yours ever
ET.

After all I stayed in in the rain & find I have read nearly all your book. You might as well ask me to write a poem myself as to write about them. Each one takes me a little deeper into a world I seem to know just for the moment as well as you — only not really knowing it I can not write. I think it is equal to 'Songs of Childhood' & 'Poems' together. It is as fresh as the first and it has the gray of the second book like gossamer over its blossom colours. I did not think one book could be so good. My favourite is 'The Dwelling Place,' if I dare commit myself.

140

'The Dwelling Place' refers to a house "named only 'Alas'."
James Milne is the editor of the Daily Chronicle.
The reversal in Thomas's and de la Mare's fortunes is acutely apparent.

Dillybrook Farm
Road
nr Bath.
28 May 1912

My dear de la Mare,

I quarter hoped to see you on Salisbury platform today. I was passing through on my way back here after a flying visit home. Did Newbolt cheer you at all? Probably not. I can't believe he is a magician. In fact I believe you are the only one within your world. Does that sound a very harsh saying? I didn't mean it so. I mean that somehow you have gone & enchanted yourself into a castle 'named only Alas!' which is a beautiful castle for me to contemplate this May in Wiltshire but a curst one to inhabit, I feel certain. Being only a reviewer I have no enchantments of any kind & won't worry you by reciting any other men's incantations such as 'Orange juice', 'Deep breathing', 'Early to bed & early to rise' etc. Being only a reviewer I feel I would endure the curse to write the poem, but that is the pathetic fallacy. It seems as if it must be so fine to write 'The Listeners'. Nobody will think it must have been fine to write my book on Swinburne. But what a pity that you can't share some of the pleasure of those who will envy you alive & even dead. Honestly, I believe it is not being 'all but old' that causes the melancholy. It is being young & old together & setting the young to judge the old instead of the other way round. Now I am entirely old. Hence this interfering letter. — I do hope there is no positive & tangible cause for your gloom, which not even Waugh could lighten. I envied him the 21/. he made out of you & cursed Milne. I get no work here at all, & shall have to make a big campaign in town next month. Probably I shall be up — & shall see you – about the middle of the month. I have been trying for librarianships but in vain.

Did you have Christian Collins' Life? I want to get hold of the story of his quarrel with Swinburne. Can you tell me about it or lend the book? I am getting on fast & shall soon be done.

I only went home because you didn't come here. I really was ready for you & would be later on, if you could manage a week end: there are sure to be cheap tickets to Westbury or Trowbridge.

Tell me you are better, & I hope the others are none the worse.

Yours & theirs ever
Edward Thomas.

141

> Dillybrook Farm
> Road
> nr Bath
> 6 June 1912

My dear de la Mare,

Many thanks for these books. Will you consent to be the 13th person I have dedicated a book to? If so my Swinburne is at your feet.

> Yours ever
> Edward Thomas.

142

This undated letter was placed at the end of the Bodleian album, but was probably written in 1912 after the publication of The Listeners.

> 13 Rusham Rd

My dear de la Mare,

Thank you for your note. My wife tells me she has an engagement on Thursday evening which prevents her from staying, & we are both sorry. But I will stay by Dick's leave. After all I shall probably not be in town tomorrow. If I am I will meet you at 6.45: otherwise I will join a Swindon train at Wandsworth Common. Your letter has gone to Davies & I hope something will come of it. By the way, Ellis was up on Tuesday & praising the 'Listeners'.

I wish I were going to be at Dillybrook farm next month if you could come, but I don't think I shall be. I mean to get over to Camden, however.

> Yours ever
> ET.

PS. My wife says she will be starting tomorrow from Wandsworth Common at 11.

143

Darrell Figgis, Irish writer and activist, worked for Dent publishers and is a fellow Bookman *reviewer.*

Wick Green
27 June 1912

My dear de la Mare,

I am glad to hear from you though it is all about me. Probably Cazenove will try Figgis. As to another suggestion for Heinemann I would gladly make one if I knew the kind of thing he might take. I am willing to do anything, but as nothing turns up the will doesn't seem much use. I am looking out for a job as secretary or librarian, & hoping I shall fail.

When will you come here? Is it possible you could manage the inside of Goodwood week, coming here on the Monday evening & returning on the Thursday morning? This is at the very end of the month. If not, do fix a date now.

Yours ever
ET.

144

De la Mare's family is on holiday in a cottage in Cowden, Kent.
Thomas's August 1912 Bookman *review of* The Listeners *observes: "Reverie has never made a more magical book than Mr. Walter de la Mare's third book of poems [...] either they take the form of childish memories or their atmosphere is like that of overpowering memory" and "of queer, half-understood or misunderstood things".*
Thomas's The Country *is published in 1913.*

Wick Green
Petersfield
22 July 1912

My dear de la Mare,

Here is a book for the children. Goodwood is next week – Tuesday to Friday. Is there any chance of your coming? I hope so. Otherwise I shall come to Cowden with Mervyn about August 20,

I expect. Please forgive anything forgivable in my Bookman notice of you – probably in the next number. I hadn't space to say more than one quarter & that seems the dullest quarter: I hope it won't seem to you unnecessary or unkind as well as dull. I am now doing the little book on the Country which is all I have in hand so far. Publishers are resolute. Editors are a little more favourable than they were, & if only the weeds would not prosper so I should be content for the time being. I expect Davies this week end. I am ever yours   Edward Thomas.

145

In a 20 August 1912 letter to his wife, Thomas records that he and Mervyn visited de la Mare in 'Cowden on Saturday'. Hodgson was also there. Thomas writes "The de la Mare's house is a pleasant one with varying views of Ashdown Forest, first a gentle meadowslope then a rising wooded ridge with a distant hill top fir clump eastwards and nearer woods more to the west. We talked comfortably about Futurists, animals etc till near midnight. De la Mare was tired and irritable and full of work. The Edinburgh Review *has asked him for a quarterly article on recent books. But what am I going to do?"*
De la Mare complains in a 5 August 1912 letter to Naomi Royde-Smith of the "ghastly tameness" of the material he sees as reader for Heinemann: "It seems as if one were continually breathing a stale slightly nauseous air. I used to think reading could do very little harm, but I don't now."

Wick Green
27 July 1912

My dear de la Mare,

I am sorry you propose not to enjoy your holiday & can't come down this week. It will be impossible for Mervyn & me to come down even as early as the 14th, I expect. At present I am practically bound until the 18th or so & should not reach you till the 22nd. Would that be too late? It may be we can start a week earlier but it is not likely. I am coming up on Wednesday for a few hours. Could you be at St George's to tea? If you can send me a card saying yes or no, please do. We have a houseful of children now — five – and are rather in their hands.

Yours ever
Edward Thomas.

146

The manuscript letter sports the pencilled date of 'Oct 1912 (?) or 4-5 Nov'.
However, Thomas's 16 August 1912 letter to Helen is written from Selsfield
House, and his 20 August 1912 letter to Helen from Coulsdon says they have
just arrived from Sevenoaks. Thomas also stayed with Ellis as a paying guest
at Selsfield House from October 1913 to January 1913, but August 1912
seems a more likely date, confirmed also by the content of Thomas's 27 July
letter to de la Mare.
Thomas was possibly on his way to visit Rupert Brooke, who continued to
lodge at Grantchester, off and on, until 1915. He had already visited Brooke
in Cambridge on a previous cycling tour with Mervyn in September 1910.

Selsfield House
Friday

My dear de la Mare

I have just got here & found this much travelled letter. I wish I
had known before. As it is I can't very well come unless we may
call – as I suggested – on Sunday on our way to Cambridge. I
should have liked a night very much: if you find a bed in a neigh-
bouring cottage for us we will stay. Mervyn may come over
tomorrow & if Ellis bicycles we might all come to tea, but I don't
think he does & at this moment he is in town. I am sorry to have
fixed up our allotted days all but Sunday & Monday like this –
Monday night we spend at Sevenoaks.

Yours ever
E.T.

Anything you suggest for Sunday ~~or Mon~~ I will adopt.

147

13 Rusham Rd   ~~WICK GREEN~~
Balham SW   ~~PETERSFIELD~~
Sunday
[postmarked 1 and 2 SP 1912]

Can we meet in town this week? I shall be at St George's on
Tuesday & Wednesday but otherwise probably fairly free till
Saturday.

E.T.

148

Thomas's use of unattributed passages from Edmund Gosse in his Swinburne *does not go unnoticed. In a letter to T.J. Wise dated 30 November 1912, Gosse writes that Thomas "is one of those people who grudge acknowledgement and he quotes metres of passages from me without mentioning my name. (He does mention it elsewhere.)"*

[postmarked SP 2 12]

It is <u>Wednesday</u> next I am up for the day. I will be at St George's anyhow. Then 2 weeks later, on the 16th. or 17th. I will come to see you. Tell me which day best suits you. I hope you will like some of Swinburne. Most of Gosse's book I did use in mine. His title is a trifle catchpenny. But I will & do not <u>complain</u> of questions if only our meetings can cease to be quarterly.

E.T.

149

De la Mare acted as reader for D.H. Lawrence's Love Poems and Others, *which he recommended for publication. Later, Thomas calls it in the April 1913* Bookman *"the book of the moment [...] as near as possible natural poetry". De la Mare also read Lawrence's new novel* Paul Morel *in the summer of 1912. Heinemann rejected it as "far too indecent". De la Mare writes to Garnett in the summer of 1912 that he didn't "feel the book as a whole comes up to Lawrence's real mark" but the "best in it is of course extraordinarily good." Duckworth published it, much altered, as* Sons and Lovers *in 1913.*

De la Mare's poetry collection Peacock Pie *comes out in midsummer 1913.* English Review *publishes Thomas's poetic essay, 'Swansea Village', in June 1914, republished in* The Last Sheaf *in 1928.*

Swansea
9 September 1912

My dear de la Mare,

I should have come on Friday if I had known before that you were not away. But I concluded you had gone as you spoke of doing. And it happened that I had booked Friday alone out of my 5 evenings. However when I have done my work here I shall be in town again — on the 16th & 17th I expect – & I may manage to see you. I expect to reach Paddington at 1 on Monday. Could we meet at lunch somewhere? If you send a word by return you will catch me a

> Poste Restante
> Amanford
> Caermarthenshire.

If you & Dick go bicycling will you call on us? We shall all be glad if you can. Garnett has mentioned Lawrence's new novel & spoken well of it but only in general terms which I have forgotten. When are your poems coming?
Tell me in good time please.
I am here writing about Swansea in the hope that the English Review will print it, for I have no other work.

> Yours ever
> Edward Thomas.

150

> Amanford
> Caermarthenshire.
> 14 September 1912

I would rather Tuesday, especially as bad weather might make Monday impossible for you. So I will wait outside the Mt Blanc in Gerrard St – about 4 doors from the Wardour St end on the right hand going toward Wardour St — at 1.30. I expect Davies will be up. My Swinburne may be out any moment with corrections & c by Secker.

> E.T.

151

An unsigned review of Thomas's George Borrow: the man and his books *appeared in the 21 September 1912* Saturday Westminster Gazette: *"Mr Thomas has written many volumes of biography, always with discernment, with a clear certainty of aim, and with a certain personal quality and tone rare in books about books. Here he had a subject after his own heart – a man greater than his books. [...] And he has put his whole skill and enthusiasm into his portrayal."*

A second review, by Claud Schuster in the 19 December 1912 Times Literary
Supplement *reads "Mr. Thomas's methods of biography are primitive",
involving "so liberal use of scissors and paste".*
Thomas's critical study on Swinburne was published in October 1912.
*Thomas is soon to start exploring his earliest experiences in pseudo-novel,
autobiography and fragmented fiction.*

Wick Green
Sunday

My dear de la Mare,

Your review was pleasant reading – I am not subtle enough to
say <u>how</u> pleasant, but very pleasant, so much so that for a time I
did not bother to think how much of it was pure kindness. After all
it is the kindness that counts & is thicker than water. I am only
sorry it was connected with haste & working against time.
However, you are at Netherhampton now & the weather could not
be better on September 22. Do you know how easy it is to get here
from Salisbury, changing at Fratton or Portsmouth? There is one
train leaving Salisbury at 12.42 getting to Fratton at 2.19, where
you have nearly an hour to wait. I wish you could come on your
way back for a night or two. I don't quite know when I shall be up
again, but very likely about the 3rd or 4th of October. Ellis has
leased 2 rooms on the ground floor at 21 York Buildings, Adelphi,
a bow windowed place just down the first road parallel to Villiers
St. He thinks of a book shop but at present takes (& gives) tea
there, & if you went to see him he would be surprised & pleased,
I think.

'Swinburne' may be out anyday now, & will be about as much
Secker's as mine, as I may have to explain to the papers, curse him.
However it may contain a dedication – rather brief – to you, & that
may rob me of a review from you, but I hope not: worse things are
done. The interesting parts of it are few, the 'signs of haste' noticed
in 'Borrow' by most reviewers are to be found there also, my haste
as well as Secker's. Just now I have no need to hasten, the only
work before me being my Reminiscences in 10 vols, and I have not
really decided to begin them before I am 42; I mean nominally 42,
I am really about 242 now, but still, for some time yet, yours (with
our love & wishes that you would appear up here)   E.T.

152

De la Mare's article on 'Current Literature' in the October 1912 Edinburgh
Review *discussed fourteen books.*
De la Mare was close to Lovat Fraser who did about fourteen Peacock Pie
*drawings in 1912. Rejected by Constable as too expensive to reproduce they
were eventually published in 1924. In 1912, de la Mare said of Fraser to
Naomi Royde-Smith that "he's a real touch of genius".*
Richard Curle is a fellow Bookman *reviewer, journalist, short story writer,
and writer on Joseph Conrad. Thomas describes his collection of stories in the
October 1912* Bookman *as a "good book", written with "gusto and precision",
and writes another favourable if muted review in the May 1914* Bookman.

Wick Green
27 September 1912

My dear de la Mare,

I wish you could have come. Time doesn't pass easily without
work except in the garden & I can't set myself to odd & speculative jobs in this uncertain state. So I should have been particularly
glad of your company. But then I daresay I should have worried
you & that you don't need. I am glad you got the 'Edinburgh'
article done & hope you will find the next one easier: you must. I
shall look forward to Fraser's illustrations. His work I admire & the
man too, but I never get anywhere near him & avoid him as far as
possible, I think. Next week I am up for several days but feel as if
we should both be uncomfortable for one another. Will you
coincide with me at all? I want to see you & if you propose a time
& place then I can almost certainly manage it. I shall be on Sunday
night at

13 Rusham Rd,
Balham

& on Monday night

c/o Richard Curle
119 Beaufort Mansions
Chelsea

Of course whenever you will & can come down we shall all
welcome you, & this is always so. Send a little notice if possible.
But we have few engagements & no time is impossible.

Yours ever
E.T.

P.S. Do you happen to have a little thing of mine called 'St David's' that I hear came out last week in the W.G.? And if so can you send it? I am very grateful for the hospitality of the W.G. & shall tempt it again.

153

Thomas's tone at the start of this letter is illuminated by his comment to Bottomley on 31 October observing that de la Mare is "'too busy" with his reviewing and publishing work, "never quite unpuckering in our scanty meetings".

Thomas's "fiction", The Happy-go-lucky Morgans, *is published in 1913.*

Thomas briefly reviews A Child's Day *in the 10 January 1913* Daily Chronicle, *calling de la Mare "the original of all singers of childhood" and writing that he "shows that his magic will survive the necessity of writing verses to pictures."*

Darrell Figgis's essays are Studies and Appreciations, *published in 1912. Thomas's assessment chimes with an earlier lukewarm review he writes of Figgis's blank verse play in the October 1911* Bookman.

De la Mare's 'The Dreamer' and 'The Quarry' appear in the December 1912 English Review.

3 November [in pencil 1912]

My dear de la Mare,

How are you & all of you? Why haven't you come down? I was in town for half a day on Wednesday but knew it was no use expecting to see you. I filled my time with editors to no very great purpose. But I have found an occupation. Every day since I got back after seeing you I have done a good bit of the fiction I was speaking of. It has no construction, progress, order or anything but trifling connections & a common centre. It will be months before it is presentable. I want a publisher to offer me something for it. Otherwise I will split it up & do what I can with the bits. — I am coming up on the 11th or so. How shall I see you? I should like to come earlier than I usually do so as not to be up late as I always have to do to see anything of you, which reduces me to what you can describe better than I can. Or will you come to town?

I have not had 'A Child's Day' yet. The D.C. & the Bookman, I think, are treating it with Children's Books, but I may get it from the English Review. My Swinburne is expected out this week.

Our cottage down at Steep is not begun yet but we are almost resolved to go into it next Spring if it is ready. I expect to [sic] live mostly or half my time at least in London, here & there.

I have been reading Figgis's essays & much impressed by his confidence & generalisation, but doubt if he is quite what he wants to be or to seem. What do you think?

    Yours ever
    Edward Thomas.

At the English Review office I heard they were going to ask you for a poem. If they haven't asked send them one.

154

A picture postcard of Paris.
Thomas suddenly went to stay with S. Jones, British representative at a French bank, a friend and colleague of Harry Hooton.
In an exchange with his wife on 15 November, Thomas refers to missed meetings with de la Mare, saying "I am sorry to lose him but I am sure I can't keep him by making all the efforts to bring off meetings myself, while he does nothing."

    c/o S. Jones Eqr,
    32 Rue des Vignes,
    Passy,
    Paris, Tuesday
    [postmarked 19 11 12]

I am here for this week, & hope I have not missed you by coming. But no word from you reached me by Monday when I left. I wrote early last week, though.

    E.T.

155

Ernest Rhys, the editor of the Everyman Library series, an important source of earnings for Thomas, who wrote introductions to several of the volumes in the series.

> Wick Green
> Petersfield
> 25 November 1912

My dear de la Mare,

I am going to be in town next week on Wednesday only for half a day so that unless you mean to be up in any case & can have tea with me I shan't see you. But the 2nd week after I shall be up for several days. What about Tuesday the 17th or would the Monday or the Wednesday be better? Let me know in good time.

I gathered the Rhyses hoped to see you last Sunday. How did you like them? I wish I could frequent those rummy gatherings with any nonchalance. I must learn if I am going to live (largely) in town next year.

I enclose a few stamps I picked up in Paris which may be new to Dick or exchangeable.

> Yours ever
> Edward Thomas.

156

This undated letter is placed near the end of the Bodleian album, but the reference to the return of a book and Tuesday the 17th suggest it comes after the 25 November 1912 letter.

> Thursday

My dear de la Mare,

I forgot this book till this evening but a day doesn't matter I expect. May I settle on coming to you on Tuesday week, the 17th. Wednesday would do as well & I would try to come early — if you aren't overbusy. Send me a card to say which day suits you: or a note, to which you might add what the fees at Whitgift are, as my plans are still in solution.

> Yours and your wife's
> ET.

157

Claud Lovat Fraser, Ralph Hodgson and Holbrook Jackson's The Sign of The Flying Fame publishing company was set up in order to make poetry accessible to the general public by means of decorative poetry broadsheets and chapbooks. Outside their own work, a James Stephens's poem was the first to be illustrated with Flying Fame. De la Mare's 'The Old Men' was the second and it sold well. When Thomas reviews Hodgson's Eve and other poems, *also produced by Flying Fame, in the October 1913* Bookman, *he notes that "the form of the book [...] is perfect".*
Percy Lubbock writes of Thomas's Swinburne *in the 5 December 1912* Times Literary Supplement *that it was "a fine achievement. There is not a sentence in his whole book which does not say something definite [...] In other words, he has grasped and held the luminous cloud which has slipped through the fingers of one critic after another". The positive reviews of* Swinburne *continue in the January 1913* Bookman *where John Freeman hails it as "the first thorough study of Swinburne".*

[postmarked DE 12 12]

Thank you.
Wednesday then – & and as early as I can.
I should think it is quite likely Stephens could be got, but I don't know him except through Bax. If the offer came through you so much the better. Rhys would know him. The Times review of Swinburne was very good.
E.T.

158

Wick Green
[in pencil, late 1912]

My dear de la Mare,
   May I remind you how willing I shall be to do anything the Times sends me, whether novels or not. I don't know if outdoor (non-technical) books, especially South of England road books & c, would be a likely class.
   I was sorry to go last night but having been 4 days in town was too tired not to want to keep it to myself. However, I hope I shall see you early in 1913 if I come up with Mervyn. I will let you know.
      Yours ever
      Edward Thomas.

159

Harold Monro's Poetry Bookshop, which went on to hold regular poetry readings, officially opened on 8 January 1913. The opening coincided with the launch at the Bookshop of Georgian Poetry 1911-1912. *Both Thomas and de la Mare reviewed the anthology, which included five poems from* The Listeners: *'Arabia', 'The Sleeper', 'Winter Dusk', 'Miss Loo', and 'The Listeners'. De la Mare gives it detailed space in his April 1913* Edinburgh Review *article, observing that "an unquestioned* seriousness *[...] is the sincere mark and claim of this anthology." and it "should at least momentarily shake the confidence of those who disparage the poetry of their own times" and highlighting specific poets and poems while omitting any reference to himself. Thomas's review in the March 1913* Bookman *is also favourable, singling out de la Mare's poems as "airiest fancy", but ends on a critical note, observing that the anthology "does not include all that is typical, or all that is best."*

13 Rusham Rd
Balham

My dear de la Mare,

Could Dick join Mervyn & me on Wednesday to see Cinderella or else the 40 Thieves – if my mother can give him a bed afterwards & let him return on Thursday morning or afternoon? I am asking her. I shall meet Mervyn at Charing X or Victoria at about 7 & Dick could join his train at the Crystal Palace if you arranged with Mervyn

c/o Mrs Harrison
 Langholen
  Edgar Rd
   Saunderstead.

I hope this can be managed & that I shall see you one day next week. I shall go to the Poetry Bookshop on Wednesday & I would be glad of your protection against hostile bards & c.

 Yours ever
  Edward Thomas

P.S. I have an additional chapter of 4 or 5 1000 words for the fiction.

160

My dear de la Mare,

Just a word to say Mervyn is coming to town next Wednesday & staying for about a week

c/o Mrs Harrison
        Edgar Rd
            Sanderstead

I should think he would be free any day (except the Thursday after) to come over to you if you wanted him or might manage a day on his way to my people towards the end of the following week.

There is rather more in Bronwen's letter than meets the eye – I don't know about your eye though. I am sorry my thoughts of your children could not get translated into something I felt sure they would like. It was impossible to send books to your house & those dry goods are becoming all my world

By the way I am not coming up with Mervyn as I had hoped. The weather makes it impossible.

Shall I send the typescript of my fiction (God bless it) straight to you? It is almost ready.

With our love to you all
        Yours ever
            Edward Thomas.

P.S. I read The Child's Day to Bronwen on Christmas day. [She'd no] fault to find with it, & said it was wonderful you could write all [that] about one child.

161

J.B. Pinker is de la Mare's literary agent.
WH is Heinemann.
Thomas refers to "bran pie" – implicitly contrasting it with de la Mare's peacock pie.
Thomas anthologises Ellis's 'Sea-country' and 'Go, nor acquaint the Rose' in Flowers I Love *in 1916. In 1946, de la Mare writes in a foreword to Ellis's* Collected Lyrical Poems *that 'Go, nor acquaint the Rose' has "never lost a syllable of its enchantment for me".*
The December 1912 English Review *prints two de la Mare poems: 'The Dreamer' and 'The Quarry'.*

Wick Green
Petersfield
3 January 1913

My dear de la Mare,
    I beg to submit & c. By this post the typescript of my fiction

goes to you. You didn't say if you wanted it direct: if you didn't or if you are too busy send it back & let me entrust it to Pinker's safe keeping in perpetuity. I want to know of course whether you would recommend it to WH & what terms he wd offer supposing he takes you seriously. But I also want to know if the various elements in it make a mere bran-pie or something like an eatable (don't bother about its being a digestible) pudding. At the present stage it seems to me goodish here, quite bad there, & on the whole lacking in architecture as the 'Standard', 'Daily News' & c say of me. It is not thorough & honest but I shan't pretend that, things being as they are, I could have done it very much better: e.g. I doubt if I could have done any good by trying to make the speeches more colloquial & more in character verbally. It strikes me that with a genius for an illustrator it might please some. What do you think about illustrations? — You see I am uncertain about a title. If you think right I will call it A True Story of Balham. In any case I thought of a foreword saying that all the characters <u>are</u> from life. — It is rather short. I don't want to add to it, but it would be possible — to the extent of 5 or 10 1000 words – if you so order – I should prefer not to put my ruinous name to it. If a publisher insists I in turn shall insist on some cash down: otherwise I will make this sacrifice at the age of 34

Send me a line saying the thing has come & where you can say anything further please do.

Shall I see you on Wednesday at Munro's 'Poetry Shop'? I think of going. Or could I see you on Monday afternoon before 4.15? If I could — & after 2.30 — send me a line by return.

I had a postcard from Henry on Xmas day, saying he was better & coming to England before very long.

I suppose you have Ellis' new poems? I like the richness & gravity of the style almost everywhere, even where they are dimmed by the Ellis moodiness — but not when the obscurity is due to bad construction as I think it sometimes is. He reminds me a bit of Sturge Moore, tho less pictorial.

We have just given notice here, but aren't settled where to go. The cottage at Steep seems likeliest. The unsettlement of these 6 months or so has almost completed my demoralisation – the last rag is that I (almost invariably) take my cold bath still. I wish myself a better new year & you too if you think it possible, things being as they are.

Yours ever
      Edward Thomas.

162

If I can come on Tuesday shall I bring Bronwen?
                                        13 Rusham Rd
                                        [postmarked 7 JAN 13]

I shall be meeting Mervyn at Victoria tomorrow at 7. His train reaches Crystal Palace at 6.32 & leaves at 6.40 so if Dick is there they could [-?-] meet. If it should turn out impossible for Dick to come will you wire here so as to reach me by 11? I will see Dick off on Thursday.
      E.T.

163

                                        13 Rusham Rd
                                        Balham
                                        [postmarked FE 3 13]

Will you look in at St George's on Tuesday at 4-5 if you are up? I begin to suppose you don't know what to say about my M.S. or haven't you had time to look at it yet. If you are in town on Wednesday I could see you anywhere you like between 2.30 and 4.30 (when I go home again).   E.T.

164

The next few letters discuss Thomas's The Happy-go-lucky Morgans.
Thomas spaces the word "impediments" as if to suggest a physical obstacle. Similarly, his spacing in the line "incomplete (excessively)" enacts the incompleteness the words call up, a quality he later celebrates in his poetry, writing to Jesse Berridge in June 1915 of the poems' "unfinish". The list in the following letter is evidence of Thomas's appreciation of balanced use of "unfinish" his sensitivity to the need for reader-accessibility; and his awareness of the need to avoid shapelessness when binding fragments loosely together with associative logic.

[in pencil, ?5 Feb, 1913]
[?15]

My dear de la Mare

Thank you. I am very sorry to hear about the children but hope when you say they <u>had</u> it badly you mean it is over. They had their party anyhow. I can almost imagine what it is like to have children sick in the house where you are working — not quite perhaps, though I have been fancying myself the most unfortunate lately. I wish I could have seen you, yet I am not fit to see anyone: have perhaps had too little exercise this filthy weather & am in consequence a sink of iniquity.

About the book. I am glad you found something good but disappointed — not surprised — you couldn't say more. I should like to know if you think there are culs-de-sac or broken threads which could be opened out or joined up. I hoped that it was not a collection of shapeless fragments tho I knew they were fragments — a not impossible compromise between a continuous fiction and a Leftaineronish group. However. The point is that I don't want to leave in things that are useless in their place. If you think there are such things & that <u>I</u> should see them I will try to amend. Otherwise let Dowling see it. I leave it to you. I have 2 further chapters, perhaps good in themselves, but only <u>impediments</u> like all the other chapters. I won't send them yet.

Of course I should like to know just what you think

useless
incomplete (excessively)
obscure
inconsistent

Has it in places a private character in a bad sense, preventing readers from sharing my knowledge, real or pretended? Does the tendency to be continuous in the last few chapters (about Philip) only show up the mass without that tendency? I can't call tomorrow: am just going home (Wednesday) & am bound to. I am hoping to get some exercise on a bicycle thro Hampshire & Wiltshire next week but am very old, about 58, but not ripe, a sort of 2nd not childhood, I don't know what.

Yours ever
Edward Thomas.

165

Thomas is writing from a house-party at Clifford Bax's house.

at the Manor House
Broughton Gifford
Wilts
19 February 1913

My dear de la Mare,

Thank you. I am away here fit for nothing but taking the air. Since hearing from you I have had a more favourable opinion from Garnett (I sent him a duplicate with additions) & he is recommending the MS to Duckworth. But if Heinemann thought well of it I should like him to have it. I feel that in such a hotch potch the variety tells & could not cut out the stories unless I had substitutes. I doubt if I have heart left to remodel entirely thro Ann even if persuaded I <u>could</u> do it.

I expect to be in town early in March, very early, & will try to arrange a meeting. I doubt if I can get to Anerley.

I am not not too <u>busy</u> for rewriting the book — I have no work — but have not life enough left in me.

Yours ever
Edward Thomas.

166

WICK GREEN,
PETERSFIELD.

My dear de la Mare,

I am getting impatient, & have been for some time. Hasn't Heinemann decided? From what you said, there was only a ghost of a chance of anything happening, & I don't believe in ghosts. A piece of news of a favourable kind would be — or might be — pleasant just now; but in any case I should like to know what W.H. thinks. I live on one or two varieties of expectation just now, but need a change of diet.

Yours ever
Edward Thomas.

Our cottage at Steep is begun so we really may move at the end of June.

167

Thomas's conception of his collection of retold proverbs, The Four-and-Twenty Blackbirds, *seems inspired by the success of de la Mare's illustrated poems, his work for children, and* A Child's Day.
The first story in Four-and-Twenty Blackbirds *is set at Broughton Gifford and the book is dedicated to Eleanor Farjeon and Clifford Bax.*

P.S. I shall be at St George's tomorrow between 4 and 5 or 6, so come in if you can.

WICK GREEN,
PETERSFIELD.
Wednesday

My dear de la Mare,

That is all right. I only hope Duckworth will like the book but when I last heard he hadn't read it. Of course I am sorry it didn't please & sorry it has added to your worries. However, I am glad to know you are going to shed them at Dillybrook Farm. I was hoping to see you there on Monday on my outward journey. As it is I will call on my way back, on the Sunday or Monday while you are there. I have already asked Mrs Couch if she will have a bed for me too. You will probably be answered by Mrs Love, who is her widow daughter, & they are apt to be slow, so you should write at once, especially as letters go more slowly in Holiday times. The station is Trowbridge, reached via Westbury. Would you like to see Bax? He is 7 miles off at

The Manor House
Broughton Gifford, Wilts.

I know he wd like to see you but have not told him you are to be there.

I will send you or Mrs Couch a card to say just when I am coming

The enclosed are some of a series of stories written (or at first planned) for children – to illustrate the birth of proverbs. If well illustrated, might a score or so make a popular book? I should like them back as soon as you have done with them.

Will you send me a card here (it will be forwarded) to say whether you are going to Dillybrook Farm? Yours ever

Edward Thomas

168

My dear de la Mare
This is to remind you of the address of

Mrs Couch

Dillybrook Farm

Road nr Bath

and to ask you to let me know when you will go so that I can fit it into my journey. I could stay a whole day & two nights I expect — about the 24th or 25th.

Yours ever

Edward Thomas

169

Thomas is cycling around the country researching for his book In Pursuit of Spring.

Salisbury

[postmarked MR 23 13]

Very glad to get your letter here & to hear you like the Proverbs. Do you mean <u>this</u> Tuesday? I might manage the Tuesday after, but am doubtful. Can you send me a word

Poste Restante

Bridgewater

Somerset

when you decide?

E.T.

Excuse this card & the hurry. Bad weather & every discomfort.

170

De la Mare was possibly preparing his article on 'An Elizabethan Poet and Modern Poetry' covering Donne and the first Georgian Poetry *anthology for the April 1913* Edinburgh Review. *De la Mare tells Nancy Royde-Smith on*

30 March that "E.T. was saying, none of the people I write about are quite solid, tangible. And how one writes is how one lives." On 1 April 1913, he writes of his and Thomas's stay together at Dillybrook Farm, "E.T. was kind and interested, as much as anyone could be but I think he was not sorry to be on his way again. People soon bore him:"
The proofs are probably of Peacock Pie.
Thomas deliberates over a number of possible illustrators for his "Proverbs" (Four-and-Twenty Blackbirds*). Eventually an edition illustrated by Ian Quillen Allan is published in 1916.*
The P S is added in pencil.

> Dillybrook Fm, Road, nr Bath.
> Sunday evening.
> [in pencil, 23 March 1913]

My dear de la Mare, It turned out so fine today that I went further than I planned & got here. They say they will be glad to have you on Friday or even on this next Tuesday if that is the day you meant – if it is, please wire the time of your train. If Mr Couch shouldn't be able to meet you at this short notice leave your things in the cloakroom & walk. Ask for the Wingfield road, then at Wingfield turn to the left on the Road, Beckington & Frome road & Dillybrook stands by some firs on the left 1 1/2 miles down.

In my hurry this morning I forgot to say how gladly I will read your proofs. If you post them on Tuesday send to Wells, Somerset (poste restante): if on Wednesday or Thursday, to Bridgewater.

I am glad you think something may be done with the Proverbs. I had thoughts of Fraser. Rackham has the advantage of being a certain seller. At home I have 2 or 3 more of the stories, & have enough in my head to make a score and of course could add to them. I think of amending some of the names, & to some extent using nursery rhyme names.

It is a lovely day & I hope you get many such here. Come not later than Friday if you can, as I should naturally be back this way about Sunday. Bax, I think, will be away in Majorca.

Mrs Couch is no letter writer so please take this as official.
> Yours ever
> E.T.

PS. Your letter just arrived. They beg me to say that either day will suit & the terms will be as for me — £1 a week.

171

The Bodleian album has the pencilled date of '1913? Summer'. However, Thomas's family went to the Norfolk coast in April 1913,Thomas staying back to write In Pursuit of Spring.
Netherhampton is the home of Margaret and Henry Newbolt where de la Mare often stayed to rest and work.
The "Rhymes" are Peacock Pie.

13 Rusham Rd
Balham S W

My dear de la Mare,

I was very sorry not to see you all last week through not remind-ing you that I was up to stay. While the rest are away at the seaside I am staying here to write my book – which I have already begun. Most days I must write, but I could manage an evening, except Tuesday, and I am free at tea time on Tuesday should you be up. If you could give me a choice of days I should be glad.

The Proverbs increase & I now have about 21, but not all copied or corrected. I hope they will be liked.

And thanks for what you say about Netherhampton. If I feel able I will take advantage of it. But travelling is apt to make me more unwilling than usual to face people.

I hope you get something from your change. The Rhymes were delicious to me & I want to have them in the book as soon as you can finish them off.   Yours ever

Edward Thomas

172

WICK GREEN,
PETERSFIELD.

My dear de la Mare

Thank you & I wish you had written before. I will try to get the rest copied in a few days & send them. They will amount I think to twenty three. It is not likely I can do more, as I am sick of them for a good reason. About terms I thought in such a case the publisher made an offer if he was really inclined to take. Won't he? If not, obviously he doesn't expect to do much with it in any case

& I would as soon he didn't have it. At the same time I want to avoid further worry & waiting & would take £25 in advance out of my royalties of 15% rising to 20% after the 3rd thousand. I believe Fraser will prove quite unsuitable as the drawings should be dramatic & he is rather strictly decorative: Hodgson agreed about this — he has mentioned it to Fraser who is quite willing to see what he could do. If he can't do what is wanted Hodgson <u>will try</u> & might do very well, I believe.

I shall be up on Tuesday. Look in at St Georges if you can? If not there I shall be <u>downstairs</u> at Ellis's (21 Adelphi Buildings) with Davies.   Yours ever

Edward Thomas

173

Duckworth publishes Thomas's book of proverbs Four-and-Twenty Blackbirds *in 1915.*

13 Rusham Rd
[in pencil, Early May 1913]

My dear de la Mare

Thank you, & I am sorry I shan't see you. Is it any use reminding you that we have a spare room this month & half of next, but not thereafter? We may move any time after Midsummer day. I should be particularly glad to see you during the fortnight after next Monday as I shall be alone.

I have copied my stories & I think they amount to 25 in all. Tell me if you like them. Then when Heinemann has decided we can discuss terms & I suppose he will write to me. If he thinks well enough of its chances to get a good illustrator I don't mind waiting — or to be accurate, I don't mind the book waiting – till 1914.

I shall be at <u>21 York Buildings</u>, Adelphi tomorrow instead of today & shall be glad if you can look in.

What about Peacock Pie? Is it done to a turn?

Yours ever

ET.

174

*Four-and-Twenty Blackbirds's 'Never Look a Gift Horse in the Mouth' is set
in 'Troy Town in Dorset'. Thomas's words to Eleanor Farjeon in June 1913
contain a reference to de la Mare: "for what you say about the Proverbs. I am
specially glad you didn't exclude the Gift Horse as Heinemann's reader does."'*

WICK GREEN,
PETERSFIELD.
23 May 1913

My dear de la Mare,

Thank you. I have at once asked Fraser to see what he can do,
to suggest a price – I couldn't. Perhaps if you send him a word he
would be likely to do a specimen or two at once? I didn't like to
suggest his hurrying. Can I alter 'Troy' I wonder? Is it clodhop-
ping or over-burlesqued?

My own feeling about Conrad is that he wouldn't. I doubt if he
has ever done anything of the kind. And then his speech has a
shade of obscurity in it. He wouldn't mind — I am sure he would
like to be asked. But if you like to be made surer than I can make
you ask Garnett, who really knows him. Personally I should incline
to ask, in order to please a good man, but I should feel certain of
being refused. Let me know if you can come & if you can jog
Fraser a little more please do — all I said was that a few drawings
might help W H to decide.

Yours ever
ET.

175

The travel book is In Pursuit of Spring.
Thomas is waiting for Heinemann's report on Four-and-Twenty Blackbirds.

[From Petersfield]
[postmarked JU 9 13]

I wish you could have come. I am just finishing the typing of a
travel book & don't feel like much of London, so I am only going
to be up for half a day on Wednesday — if you are up come to St

George's at 4 - 5. But I am sorry you get no luck. W H's report will be welcome whatever it is.   E.T.

176

The 4 January 1913 Saturday Westminster Gazette *sports a review of Thomas's* Swinburne: *"Mr Thomas writes fully in this brief and yet comprehensive study. He neither forces his material to his own ends nor shrinks from absolute frankness."*
Theresa Whistler records that in June de la Mare was staying alone at Edith Sichel's house in Hambledon Hurst, 10 miles from Dene cottage finishing his long article 'Current Literature' for the July 1913 Edinburgh Review. *This article discussed nine books of prose, poetry and biography, including work by Arthur Benson, Henry James and Alice Meynell.*
To save money, Thomas was moving into a smaller cottage in Steep.
He had just finished writing In Pursuit of Spring.

> Sunday
> [postmarked 15 JU]
> [in pencil, 1913]

My dear de la Mare, Your review in the W.G. gives me enormous pleasure in spite of the thought that you must have had to read such a lot of the book! I am sure I should not have enjoyed it any more if I had deserved it.

I wasn't a night in town so your lettercard didn't reach me for a day or two. In any case I left at 6.40 & couldn't have come round. Are you going to be in town anytime on Tuesday, if you are will you send a card to 13 Rusham Rd Balham? If I stay up Wednesday night I would come to you if you were free, but I am keeping as much as possible out of London in this fine weather. Although I make precious little out of it here. We don't expect to move now before the end of the month & lack of water at the new place may keep us out till August.

Have you done your Edinburgh article & if so could you spend a few days walking about anywhere or come here or come down to Dillybrook Farm? I've no right to go except that I have just finished an itinerary almost as tedious as the Icknield Way & I always pretend I ought to have a rest after a book. Let me know.

By the way I'm clearing out a good few of my books & I want to give you either J. A. Symonds' 'Greek Poets', or 12 vols. of Swift

(1750), or a complete 'Spectator' (modern), or Jowett's Plato's 'Republic', or Clarendon's 'Great Rebellion'. Tell me which.

Fraser's price is certainly low. I hope something is going to happen now. Yours ever ET.

177

On the blue envelope of the pink paper of this letter is written "very special | precious".

De la Mare's Peacock Pie *was published at midsummer. Many of the poems were written around midnight after working all day as a reader for Heinemann. As already noted, Theresa Whistler reports that de la Mare's recipe for writing such poems was "Get very tired first".*

"Magic hath stolen away" is a line from 'The Truants'.

"Coo-ee" is from 'Longlegs', a Peacock Pie *poem about Thomas that describes him hallooing "coo-ee" across the combe near his home in Steep.*

Clifford Bax's house in Broughton Gifford.

Monday
[postmarked JU 24 13]

My dear de la Mare

Your book has caught me up on my travels. I shall cut it tomorrow night, I hope, at an inn at Salisbury. I promise it to myself as I should strawberries & cream, liver & bacon, or Salad Gruyère & home made bread. And it is just as definite a pleasure. If I had to imagine a book to fit your title I should imagine your book; at least I should imagine something which only your book would embody. I love it & I think not the less because 'Magic hath stolen away' all of me that could feel such things without your help. Hudson's are the only other living man's books that give me such perfect pleasure, with its edge perhaps a little keener for the faintest taint of envy. I hope some paper will give me a chance of saying this in some more tedious & roundabout way.

I am now four days away from home but expect to be back on Wednesday. My wife says we are really about to move. I shall be very busy finally arranging what to get rid of, so please remind me what I shall send you, if you would like any of those books I mentioned. Probably I shall be in London in a fortnight's time & will try to see you, but can hardly get to Anerley as my only evening is booked. Could I see you in town anytime on Wednesday or Thursday the 9th or 10th?

I met a countryman yesterday who had twice <u>seen</u> ghosts & once <u>heard</u> them, five voices singing & feet dancing. You should have seen him take his oath. Magic had stolen away half his 'wits': he foamed slightly & his eyes started.

Yours ever

E.T.

Coo-ee

~~I write from Bax's house~~

178

'The Gnomies', included in the 1902 Songs of Childhood, *is dropped from the revised second edition of 1916.*
The title page of The Happy-go-lucky Morgans *includes a quotation from Thomas Hardy's 'Julie-Jane'.*

Wick Green

[postmarked JU 29 13]

My dear de la Mare,

Did you really mean me to suggest meddlings with 'Songs of Childhood'? I had a sort of hope you would send me a copy to mark (whereby I should have two copies) so that I put off the evil hour. However, if you are to cut out some I suggest 'The Gnomies', 'Bluebells' (& yet should like to keep them), 'Song', 'The Fairies Dancing', 'The Pilgrim', 'The Gage', 'The Raven's Tomb' (tho I do not propose to black it out of my copy belonging to 1902, the days when Nevinson was literary editor at the D.C.). All I did on Tuesday night was to cut Peacock Pie & put in my thumb here & there, with an idea of taking a few lines for the title page of my fiction which is now in the proof stage.

Yours ever   ET.

179

Thomas was considering both Fraser and Eleanor Farjeon's friend Rosalind Thornycroft as possible illustrators of Four-and-Twenty Blackbirds.

~~WICK GREEN~~,   Steep (after
~~PETERSFIELD.~~   Friday D.V.)
[in pencil, just before Sat 5 July 1913]

My dear de la Mare

This is in the muddle of the semifinal. We expect to move on Saturday & I shall be up on Wednesday after (the 9th). If you can be in town then I hope you will come to St George's. I will let you know later <u>when,</u> because I have engaged myself for the Russian ballet, & it may be a matinee.

I'll send a word to Hodgson but can't hope he'll be able to send anything in by Thursday. Meantime a Miss Rosalind Thorneycroft I know is meditating an attempt on illustrating 2 or 3 & if she comes off I will show you, that is supposing everything isn't already off – or on.

There's nothing in my head to ache but I don't congratulate you. I only wish you had come over Salisbury Plain with me last week, then you would not have had a headache. Still one can't work <u>and</u> ride over Salisbury Plain. Plato I fear won't console you, but I send him for what he's worth.

Yours ever
     Edward Thomas

I shall be up on the Tuesday too, from 4 to 6 or so at St George's

180

Discussion continues on the illustrations for Four-and-Twenty Blackbirds. *Thomas writes on* Peacock Pie *in the September 1913* Bookman.

13 Rusham Rd

My dear de la Mare

Your letter had to be forwarded & didn't reach me in time. Are you free this afternoon? If I call at Heinemann's at 3.30 can you come to tea? Anyhow I will & you might leave word for me if you've gone. Are you free on Sunday? I could come over from 12 to tea time. Send me a card will you? Hodgson doesn't like to do anything till Fraser understands definitely which apparently he did not when they last met. There's no reason why both Hodgson & Miss Thorneycroft shouldn't both send drawings. Miss

Thorneycroft talks of doing some very soon. Have you met her –
a daughter of Hamo Thorneycroft?

> Yours ever
> ET.

Please <u>tell Constables to send Peacock Pie to the D.C.</u> They
positively have not.

181

> Wick Green (& here till about Thursday.)
> [postmarked JY 6 13]

If you can be at St George's on <u>Wednesday at 4</u> will you send me
a word to 13 Rusham Rd by return? On Tuesday I find I have
hardly any time but all Wednesday afternoon.

> ET.

182

*This postcard has no date but in a 20 August 1913 letter to Freeman, written
from near Norwich, Thomas asks to stay Saturday night. This was probably
his first overnight stay with the Freemans.*

> 13 Rusham Rd.

I have stayed here after all & perhaps missed a letter from you. In
case you propose Saturday or Sunday, I can't come on Saturday
but will on Sunday, or if you say Monday, Monday it shall be. I
hope I am not putting you out by not getting your letter: should it
be forwarded here from Freeman's I will write again, if this does
not answer it.   E.T.

183

*The H's are probably Thomas's friends the Hootons. The Icknield Way was
published in August 1913.*

> 13 Rusham Rd
> Balham SW.

My dear de la Mare,

I should like to come over on Sunday about tea time, but at no exact hour as I shall cycle & it might be wet & c. But not later than 6. I am glad you have got the Icknield Way. No I know that the H's are not nursing wrath but they may have an idea that you are — only they don't allow themselves to worry much about what anyone thinks or feels.

Yours ever

ET.

Section III
1913-1917 Two Poets

In September 1913 Thomas records an aborted attempt at composing a poem in a letter to de la Mare that shows intense interest in and awareness of the poetic composition process. De la Mare helps Thomas come out of a serious depression, and assists him in getting reviewing work from the *Times* and in obtaining a Royal Literary Fund grant. Thomas continues his experiments in prose writing, moving from retold proverbs to a second fiction, exploring different approaches to writing methods, and celebrating rather than fighting his propensity to take on a loose structure.

At the end of 1914 and start of 1915 both de la Mare and Thomas are confined at home. Separately, they experience a surge in creativity, resulting for both men in the production of a large number of poems. In 1915 de la Mare becomes a fellow of the Royal Society of Literature, while Thomas decides to enlist. De la Mare is made a beneficiary of the proceeds of Rupert Brooke's writings, resulting in an American lecture tour in 1916. Thomas goes to France in January 1917, before de la Mare returns from America, and is killed at the Front in April 1917.

184

De la Mare had been in St Merryn between Newquay and Padstow, visiting J.D. Beresford, the writer, dramatist and journalist. Beresford was a friend of D.H. Lawrence, who stayed in Beresford's cottage in Cornwall
Cornwall gripped de la Mare's imagination in his writing from this time on. The White Horse pond refers to Cowden, as Thomas's 20 August 1912 letter to Helen reveals: "Mervyn went to Cowden on Saturday and had an afternoon's roach fishing with the de la Mare's. [...] The pond is a little one full of roach by the White Horse on the Common almost spoilt by golf."

13 Rusham Rd
Balham SW.
Tuesday
[in pencil, end of Aug 1913]
[26?]

My dear de la Mare,

Your twice forwarded letter has only just this morning reached me, & I am now booked for the whole day. I wish I had known, for I should very much have liked to come. Since I saw you I have been mostly away from London & from home, & tomorrow I am taking Mervyn & Bronwen to Flansham near Bognor for a week or ten days: after which I have promised to go to Ellis, that is on about the 5th of September. But if you are still there on the 5th I think I could get one day with you. Will you let me know at

    c/o Mrs Bryan
      Flansham Lane
        Flansham nr Bognor.

There is no news about the Proverbs. Miss Thorneycroft prefers to get married. Another lady has some of the proverbs to consider, but though I do what I can I rather doubt if anything will happen.

Did Cornwall do you any good? I hoped to see you or hear from you before this. I do hope you find some rest, & especially sleep, at Cowden.

I don't think I had a notice of Peacock Pie in the D.C. I have not seen one by me anywhere. They delay so: have only this day printed a tiny notice on Bridges I did before Christmas.

We are rather scattered. My wife is in Switzerland for 3 weeks with a sister. Baby is with another sister. I keep one or both the elder children in tow.

Tell me if about the 5th is not impossible. You are too far for me to reach from Flansham or I could come before for a day.

I am sorry not to be there today especially as I have not been able to let you know before. My love to you all,

    Yours ever
      ET.

Are the fish grown in the White Horse pond? Dick knows, I expect.

185

Placed about a month later in the Bodleian album, but the references to Mervyn and Godwin suggest that this was written before 5 September. Thomas wrote a letter to Eleanor Farjeon from 'Godwins' on 5 September, making

travel plans that included his son Mervyn.

My dear de la Mare,

Is it any good my coming down to you by a morning train to Cowden on Friday & then leaving you for Ellis' that evening? As I have Mervyn to meet then I can't well stay the night, & the same would apply on Saturday or Sunday unless you could put us both up on one of those nights. Will you send me a card by return to reach me on Thursday night if possible

   c/o Godwin Baynes
      30 Victoria Park Square
        Bethnal Green   E.
If I don't hear then I shall go straight to Ellis at
      Selsfield House
        East Grinstead
and look out for a card from you there.
      Yours ever
        Edward Thomas
If Friday suits what trains are there from London Bridge or Victoria?

186

W. H. is Heinemann.

St George's
Thursday
[postmarked SEP 4 13]

Thank you for your letter suggesting today & Saturday, & crossing my note. Today was impossible. I will try to get Ellis along on Saturday but its an awkward journey, isn't it, except on a bicycle. If I hear from you that you are free on Friday I shall come down by a train reaching Cowden at 12.48: but now I remember you spoke of being at W.H's on Fridays. I have just brought Bronwen in to join baby at an aunt's.
        E. T.

187

Placed in the manuscript between October 1913 and January 1914 letters, this account of Thomas's attempt at poetry was probably written on 7 September 1913 during his brief stay at Selsfield House. His essay 'Insomnia' in The Last Sheaf, *which writes up the episode in detail, dates the attempt as occurring on the seventh of September. References in other September 1913 letters to de la Mare confirm this.*

Thomas's application of Pope's denigratory "mob of gentlemen" to poets such as de la Mare who show facility with rhyme, foreshadows his own preference for looser manipulation of rhyme, as in his poetry from 1914 on.

SELSFIELD HOUSE,
EAST GRINSTEAD.
Sunday

My dear de la Mare

I am sorry about today. Ellis couldn't come because his wife's bicycle was useless & we couldn't hire one. Well, I started before 3, got a puncture in a mile, mended it, but in getting the tyre back ripped the tube, returned here & mended that, started again after 4 & found my tyre flat at the point I had reached before. So I could not come & was sick with, & soon afterwards sick of, myself. I am very sorry to have had you expecting me vainly. However, I have written to my wife about next Sunday & we will let you know as soon as we can what can be done. I hope your wife has got over the packing & the return without too much trouble.

This address will most likely find me till Saturday morning, tho it is not the time & place to do nothing in, which is all I have to do, except that in sleepless hours this morning I found myself (for the first time) trying hard to <u>rhyme</u> my mood & failing very badly indeed, in fact comically so, as I could not complete the first verse or get beyond the rhyme of ember & September. This must explain any future lenience towards the mob of gentlemen that rhyme with ease.

        Yours ever
        Edward Thomas

188

Thomas wrote a strikingly joyful review of Peacock Pie *for the September 1913* Bookman: *"what good pastry, and what peacock flesh, succulent and spicy, Mr. de la Mare does bake – he do." He highlights 'Miss T' and 'Nobody*

Knows', writing that de la Mare "is a master, is the master, in this style." He also singles out 'The Horseman' and 'The Huntsmen', and takes the opportunity to praise de la Mare's 'unrivalled romance', The Three Mulla-Mulgars, *to quote from his 'Bunches of Grapes' from* Songs of Childhood, *and to praise the "silvery wings" of* The Listeners, *concluding that "I am content to travel any part of England or no man's land with this poet".*

STEEP,
PETERSFIELD.
18 September 1913

My dear de la Mare,

I saw my agent in town before I left & he seemed hopeful of doing something with my Proverbs which I spoke of. He says publishers as a rule don't like to have to consider a book already provided with illustrations. So I suppose this only confirms the impression that W.H. does not much want them. Unless you think he does will you send them on to me, & I will revise them & put them in the agent's hands?

I hope you haven't found my attempts to praise Peacock Pie as it deserves too sugary, & still more that you didn't suspect anything Parthia[n] in the illcalculated epithet featherwe[ight]

Yours ever
E.T.

189

'Ecstasy' was intended for an essay series to be published by Batsford. Thomas never finished it.
Munro is Harold Munro.
The MSS is Four-and-Twenty Blackbirds.
The image of feathers blowing down reappears in Thomas's poem 'Snow', composed on 7 January 1915.

STEEP,
PETERSFIELD.
24 September 1913

My dear de la Mare

No it didn't tire me & if it did it would be without resentment. I suppose country habits & the custom of going early to bed after fairly hard days of walking or riding makes me rather useless after 10, or it may be simple mental infecundity. I shall come again as soon as I can, perhaps Monday Oct 6th, which at any rate is the earliest possible day. Till then I am here writing about Ecstasy, good Lord, but spending the Saturday & Sunday nights (4th & 5th) at Munro's.

Thank you for what you have done with W.H., & I will wait the 2 weeks. Even if he decides to keep the MSS I assume he will not object to my serialising – it is just possible I could do so, & I have some small confidence in the little things. They are not feather-weight though. I believe you take the featherweight as my label. I thought rather of snow feathers coming down from above not bantam or goose feathers blown up & down again. So I should have said gossamer, which has an earthly conception but a heavenly generation. I wish I could say how much I like it, but simple things are beyond my saying. Well, I am glad you have liked the years as I have liked the gossamers & their autumns, & something more than that too, at Anerley & Harting & Cowden. Good luck.

Yours ever
E.T.

190

A. Martin Freeman was a university friend of Thomas's and became an authority on Irish literature and Gaelic folk-songs; Feminine Influence *is dedicated to him.*

13 Rusham Rd
Balham SW.
Thursday
[postmarked OC 2 13]

My dear de la Mare,

Shall I come on Monday night joining you at Victoria at 7 or so? But if Saturday would be better I might manage it – I am not going to be at Munro's – or even Sunday. Let it be Monday if possible. Can you send a card here by return as I may only just call here for letters tomorrow morning & not be here again till Monday. Should this reach you too late for that you could get me through

A Martin Freeman
166   Lauderdale
Mansions
Maida Vale   W.
        Yours ever
            Edward Thomas

191

*A certain purchase refers either to opium or a revolver. 'The Attempt',
published in* Light and Twilight, *tells the story of a suicide attempt.
Thomas first met Robert Frost on 6 October 1913.*

13 Rusham Rd
Balham.
6 October 1913

My dear de la Mare,

I don't know how much I have to thank you before & can't
nicely distinguish between post & propter but certain it is that this
morning I hadn't more of my original design left than to make (I
think largely for form's sake) a certain purchase. I wish I could
have seen you again. I was a nuisance, I know. But I can at any rate
write something better now than 'The Attempt'. Your letter when
I found it here at 7 finally disarmed me. I feel a fool, a sort of wise
fool, — not one of your best creations, — with not a shred of
peacock about me, — but such as it is, it thanks you for its
existence, & it will try & do 2200 words by the 15th & if it resembles its former self certainly will do them. It hopes the books will
come soon. It will also try to stay here instead of hurrying to the
Pump[?] in the Nation Street, its ultimate home, where it will no
doubt pooh-pooh the existence of Steep, Anerley, & the like if it
has the chance.

Yours ever
Edward Thomas

Shall I really try the story you sketched?

192

*Written in pencil.
In this reference to a possible suicide attempt, the "Saviour" is either a revolver
or opium.
Heinemann are considering* Four-and-Twenty Blackbirds *again.*

Monday
[postmarked OCT 6 13]

My dear de la Mare
Thank you for what you said last night. I think I have now

changed my mind though I have the Saviour in my pocket. The final argument was my mother who has received nearly all the other blows possible. I very much hope you did not take me quite as seriously as I did myself. — I should be glad if Heinemann would not keep me waiting uncertain while he finds an artist.

Yours ever   E.T.

193

Thomas is still considering the possibility of Fraser illustrating Four-and-Twenty Blackbirds

Steep
Wednesday [postmarked OCT 8 13]

Just got your letter. Thank you. I would like the Supps. containing reviews of novels. But the books haven't come yet. I'm just off to look for them at the station. I heard from Fraser too & couldn't go – I mentioned the stories in replying. Excuse a great hurry. E.T.

194

Helped by de la Mare, Thomas was hoping to get work writing for the Times.

Steep
10th [in pencil, Oct 1913]

My dear de la Mare, This is good news & I am glad to have it at your hands. Thank you also for the supplements. The novels have come & it is a job reading them. Reading from 9 a.m. to 12 p.m. (with only one interval for supper) I only did a novel & a half: I find I must read every word. However. It must be the excuse for this note.

I will write to Heinemann. Fraser I shall make a point of seeing for an hour when I am next up. When I come to you I would rather have you & not him, if I may choose. I will let you know when I can be up again. At present I think I am safest working all the time & I have several things I can get on with. But I expect it will be before the end of the month that I get to town.

Yours ever
E.T.

195

Many reviews of Thomas's Walter Pater: A Critical Study *were damning. The 11 October 1913* Saturday Westminster Gazette *review begins "Mr. Thomas seems mainly concerned to appear the clever critic and to belittle Walter Pater", his book is "too patronising" and includes "many covert sneers and slighting passages." In the 23 October* Times Literary Supplement, *J.C. Bailey writes that Thomas "has no inward understanding of Pater's attitude towards life, and no intellectual ear for what was fine and rare in his method of writing [...] [and] has no business to be writing a book about Pater." Another somewhat critical review by T.E. Page, appears in the* Bookman *in November 1913.*

STEEP,
PETERSFIELD.
26 October 1913

My dear de la Mare,

Thank you. Then I will come on Tuesday as soon after 7 as I can. I am sorry to hear you aren't to do the Fairy tales, for of course those terms are absurd. But won't you do them in any case? You would most likely find places for some if not all in the 'English Review' & c. If you can do them, you should. When they are done you will perhaps make better terms, or not need better, if you have sold them serially. I wish you would do them.

I am longing for something to do to prove to myself that I can do — something.

There is now a hitch over the Proverbs. Heinemann's agreement said payment on publication. I had suggested & now expect payment on my final revision & completion of the MS, that is in a few days after getting it back. I do hope this won't upset everything.

Do you really think Pater good? The only review I have had was a malevolent contemptuous (unreasonable) one in the 'Saturday'. I am afraid it's formless & does not admit as it ought to that Pater is good of his kind, & wastes too much time in trying to prove the kind bad.

No. Nothing more from the 'Times'. But there is a chance of an outdoor book to do – that about the part of Wales I know best – which sounds too good to be possible.

Yours ever
E.T.

196

Thomas was staying as a paying-guest with Ellis at Selsfield House in order to write.
Bruce Richmond in the editor of the Times Literary Supplement.

> Steep
> [in pencil, end of Oct 1913]

My dear de la Mare,

I am leaving home for a time next week & going to work at Ellis's while I look for rooms in that neighbourhood. I must be out of town, yet not too far, not quite away from everyone. Now if things were not as they are – and indescribable by the pen that has lately written a bad article for Richmond (vanity compels me to say I know exactly how bad) — I should propose most infallibly to come & see you on Tuesday next. But I know I might not come. So this is to ask if I may turn up, as I certainly will if I can? Of course if I feel differently nearer the day I will send a card. This is a 2nd attempt to write something not cryptic or too damned incontinent. Is it possible you would be in town on Tuesday or Wednesday? I feel now so almost certain of being afraid to come to your house.

> Yours ever
> E.T

197

Thomas reviewed John Halsham's Kitty Fairhall *in the 12 December 1901* Daily Chronicle *and his* Lonewood Corner *in the 9 May 1907* Morning Post.
Thomas is writing a book on Keats.

> at Selsfield House
> E Grinstead
> Thursday

My dear de la Mare

I do know John Halsham's Books – Idlehurst, Kitty Fairhall, Lonewood Corner. (I hear that he lives nearby.) I think perhaps I could do better with his new book (which I have not seen yet) than with those novels. This morning's Times shows that somebody else had to write the article after all. Your letter mitigated the effect of this discovery. But I now repeat all blows, real & imaginary, past & present & future, as if I were a machine to exhibit that state of mind, or absence of mind; & it will need some accident & that pretty forcible and not long delayed to get me on another track. Along this one there is only one stopping place, where you go over the edge. I am sorry I can't keep it to myself better, but thats the disease. Perhaps if I alienate everybody thoroughly & have to stand alone I shall really discover a way of doing so. Don't begin, will you?

I wrote at once to my wife about the servant & hope something will come of it. Is your wife's eye quite well again?

The books have come from the London library. Can you lend me yet another — perhaps you have it yourself —

Ernest de Selincourt's edition of Keats' Poems (Methuen) The notes if I remember rightly are valuable.

Yours ever
ET.

198

Clement King Shorter's 1913 George Borrow and his circle *included unpublished letters from and to Borrow.*
Halsham's book of country essays, Old Standards south country sketches, *was published in London in 1913, some pieces having been previously printed in the* English Review. *The book follows a format Thomas knows well.*

at Selsfield House

My dear de la Mare
Practically the only new things in Shorter are letters to his wife & stepdaughter & of these the most interesting those from Hungary in 1844. The other unpublished MSS — verse translations & the Manx diaries – which he's got hold of are to be reserved to make additional volumes in Collected Works. 2 vols. of verse translations! There are some reminiscences not in other books on pp. 416-419. The book should have been a brochure of 20pp. just containing the documents.

I am pretty sick over Heinemann. Largely its my fault for my
irritable tone all along. If he had asked me to let him see my next
book I should not have thought twice about it, but he shoved it in
without a word. So tho I said at the beginning of the correspondence I wanted the money more or less at once. He evaded
answering & then shoved the condition – payment on <u>publication</u>
– into the agreement. I didn't want any more rejected MSS now.
Constables have just finally decided not to give terms that would
make it possible for me to do a book on S.W. Wales we have been
discussing. But I take it its no use either reopening with W.H. or
saying the sort of thing I could say in return for making my brain
boil impotently this morning. curse him.

Richmond sent Halsham's book & I shall do it soon. Its rather
moderate stuff, mixed idyllic & realistic, the mad university man's
country commentary. But I suppose I must be moderate on this
line.

I suppose you haven't got de Selincourt's Keats? If you could
send it, it would be very useful. But I have actually got the book in
hand now. I try hard to keep on reading & writing, but every now
& then my will gets a paralytic stroke & I am a corpse except for
wretchedness. If I can get the thing done by the end of next week
I hope to see you soon after.

Yours ever

Edward Thomas

199

13 Rusham Rd   ~~STEEP~~

Balham, SW   ~~PETERSFIELD~~

2 January 1914

My dear de la Mare,

I am applying to the L.C.C. for a temporary lectureship at their
'Non-Vocational Institutes' where people are to be 'informed &
convinced that life is more than livelihood', etc.. I suggest as
subjects Gilbert White, Richard Jefferies, Borrow, Keats, &
Modern Poetry. The application has to be sent in at once. Could
you give me one of the 3 necessary testimonials — only a few
words?

I am going to be in town next week. Is there any time or place before Thursday where I could see you in town?

Yours ever

E.T.

200

The year of this letter is misdated. It was probably written on 4 January 1914 since Thomas's Walter Pater *was published at the end of 1913. Also the first number of* The New Statesman *was published in April 1913, and this poem of de la Mare's was published in the 13 September 1913 issue:*

> *There once was an old, old woman,*
> *Who lived in a very old shoe,*
> *And she had such numerous, though beautiful children*
> *She didn't know what to do.*
>
> *So she gave them copies of the Spectator,*
> *And told them to regard themselves as fed;*
> *And when they complained, she cried aloud in her anger:*
> *You shall have the* Nineteenth Century *as well, she said.*

This poem is not printed elsewhere. It refers to de la Mare's first leading article for the Times Literary Supplement, *2 March 1911, on the history of* The Spectator. *Thomas would have appreciated this since he helped with the research, sending de la Mare relevant texts in a February 1911 letter.*

The 3 January 1914 New Statesman *had an unsigned lukewarm review of Thomas's* Pater. *It starts by declaring: "It is a pity that Mr. Thomas is so indefinite in his charmingly written study of Pater, for if there is a man of letters it is possible to estimate, it is surely that academic aesthete", and ends: "endeavours to carve cameos the size of the Elgin Marbles can never be pursued with success."*

De la Mare's 'The Enchanted Hill' appears in Poetry and Drama.

A. Martin Freeman lived at Lauderdale Mansions.

13 Rusham Rd

Balham S W

4 January 1913 [1914]

My dear de la Mare

Thank you for the epitaph or testimonial, & for the two letters. I wish I had got the one at Christmas. But I will be at Pecorini's on

Tuesday. I shall be free at 7 – in case you are also will you suggest a place for that hour. St George's if you like. I shall be tomorrow night almost certainly at

166 Lauderdale Mansions
Maida Vale W.

I am up with Bronwen for a few nights. My wife is staying on at Selsfield because Baby is too unwell to move. The poor child has a cold & a boil & is altogether sick of things except stories & lullabies. I hope you all got safe through the dangers of Christmas

Your notice of Pater in the W.G. was by far my best & I should think it was as interesting to the ordinary reader as to me. Also I like a 'New Statesman' short poem a little while ago: &, but rather less, a longer one in 'Poetry & Drama'.

Yours ever
E.T.

Yes I returned the L.L. books long ago. Many thanks.

201

At Selsfield House
East Grinstead
7 January 1914

My dear de la Mare,

I am sorry to say I am not going to apply for that lectureship. It was quite a brief attack of imaginary courage that made me think of it. All day yesterday I was coming to the conclusion that — as I felt when first I saw the advertisement — I could never face an audience. So bang goes your ink & paper, also Hudson's, Garnett's, & Seccombe's, & mine also in ridiculous apology. If it were not for having troubled you I should really be feeling elated at having escaped that particular form of nightmare.

But I shall suggest coming to see you now & then until I have somewhere where you can come to see me.

Yours ever
ET

202

Writer and editor Clifford Bax lived at 11 Luxembourg Gardens. Thomas later dedicates Four-and-Twenty Blackbirds *to him and Eleanor Farjeon. Thomas reviewed John Halsham in 1901, 1907 and now again in the 13 November 1913* Times Literary Supplement.
Thomas's income was in part derived from the sales of review copies.

> Selsfield House
> East Grinstead
> 12 January 1914

My dear de la Mare

For me it was impossible. I wish it were February 5th for your sake.

I never heard any suggestion of Coleridge falling in love with Dorothy Wordsworth, but there were passages in her journals which made me think she might have been in love with him.

On Friday everyone leaves here & I am going to be at

> 11 Luxembourg Gardens
> Brook Green, W..

but may be home for the week end to clear the books & c from my old study. But I don't know. I am all right as long as I succeed in just writing or walking or smoking, yet have qualms when I do succeed. I don't like demi-sponging any better for seeing the whole hog as a possibility not far hence.

The Times sent Halsham & I did hi[m ?] & they printed the column: then 3 books to do together & the review was printed a week or 2 back. But several trifles — due to their neglecting what I told them about my address, & not telling me they wanted those novels back (do they expect all review books back?) – make me suppose they won't trouble me again.

I don't know how long I shall be in town, – not longer than I must while I look for a place in the country somewhere, — but I hope to see you. Ellis & I will be at St George's on Friday at 4 & should like to see you: also on the following Wednesday. For a time I must work in the evenings.

I am glad Mervyn went to see you. He was at a loose end for days. I don't see him changed, but fathers don't see.

Yours ever

E.T.

203

Harry Hooton, Thomas's long-term close friend.

> 11 Luxembourg Gardens
> Brook Green W.
> 23 January 1914
> [postmarked JA 24 13]

My dear de la Mare,

I am going to walk with Hooton, I hope, on Sunday the 1st of February. Shall I come to you on the Saturday for supper <u>and</u> breakfast? or have I made breakfast impossible? He that will not when he may he shall not when he would. But I would. As to Ellis, I think he must have gone to Switzerland & I don't know his plans. I know he would have come.

I am here for a doubtful number of weeks. In fog & frost it is one of the worst places hidden from the sun. No brook. The green all white, & the white dirty.   Yours ever

E.T.

Ellis's address is
13 Addison Rd North, Holland Park, W.

204

Thomas writes in a 20 September 1913 letter to his agent Cazenove: "I am thinking of a fiction to use some of my travel notes." He works on it in the first half of 1914 and then abandons it as "tedious".
While Thomas has found he lacks the courage to lecture, de la Mare successfully delivers his first lecture, on 'Magic in Poetry', at Leeds University, declaring that "all experience is a conflict between realities" and in the highest state of poetry "beauty – even earthly beauty – becomes only a promise or a memory, the symbol of a remote reality".
Conrad is Joseph Conrad.

> 11 Luxembourg Gardens
> Brook Green W.
> 11 February 1914

My dear de la Mare,

I am going to try another fiction of a less organic kind & am asking the Royal Literary fund to do something to help me by a grant. Garnett has already approached the secretary & I have filled up the form of application & sent in the enclosed letter. I need another letter from a 'respectable person authenticating the merits of the case.' Will you write it to

The Secretary
   Royal Literary Fund
     40 Denison House
       206 Vauxhall Bridge Rd
         Westminster   SW.
I should be grateful if you would.

I looked in vain for a report of your lecture, but I suppose it was delivered. I should like to read it.

At present I am uncertain whether I shall go home or elsewhere to write my book. If I can see you early next week I should be very glad & will try. But I have to go here & there to see Conrad and others & may not manage it.

       Yours ever
        Edward Thomas.

205

In a 22 February letter to Eleanor Farjeon, Thomas refers to receiving "a batch of books from the Westminster by de la Mare's intercession". He reviews four books on Irish song and poetry, in the 21 March 1914 Saturday Westminster Gazette.
Thomas's prose piece 'The Inn by the Aspen', is published in the 4 July 1914 Saturday Westminster Gazette. *It bears similarities to his later poem, 'Aspens', composed on 11 July 1915.*

                 Steep
                 Petersfield.
                 22 February 1914

My dear de la Mare,

Thank you for the Lit. Supp. (which I have drawn on shame-lessly) and for letting me see Newbolt's letter. It is very kind of him. I was very glad to hear that you are threatening Heinemann, because I think you ought to & believe you can with impunity. Will you let me know how you prosper? Since we met I have had the story as much as possible in my mind. It suits me better than the other — I only hope not too well, I mean so well that it will encourage my usual rather self indulgent easy methods. But I will report when there is anything to report. I hope to see you when I am up, which will probably be in two or three weeks hence. In spite of rain & snow I am glad to be here again.

Yours ever
Edward Thomas

P.S. Miss Royde Smith sent the batch of Irish bards this morning. I like her better than I like them.

206

Thomas received a grant from the Royal Literary Fund.

Steep
26 February 1914

My dear de la Mare

I was very glad to find your telegram waiting for me when I came down from my study to dinner — and more glad that you send the telegram than that the RLF are sending £150, which, in fact, has so far meant nothing at all to me. But I will not attempt any further description or explanation. What will perhaps please you more is that I have actually begun that fiction, or a fiction: begun it very easily & lazily & anyhow, for the hope of really getting into the subject later.   Yours ever   E.T.

207

The "stories of the English travellers" eventually becomes A Literary Pilgrim in England, *published by Methuen in 1917.*
Thomas's article 'The Vogue of the Road Book' in the 28 March 1914 New Statesman *is critical of "modern road books" of which he wrote a number himself. Often, he observes, "the part is greater than the whole".*

Steep
Petersfield
17 March 1914
[postmarked M 18 14]

My dear de la Mare,

I expect to be in town for a night or 2 next week. Shall I come to you on Monday or Tuesday night? If so you might tell me which best suits you. I have been working daily at the fiction since we met but so far have done nothing I am pleased with & the MS is too bad to show you any of it. Other work is very scarce. I have undertaken to write some stories of the English travellers for the Oxford Press, using Hakluyt & c. Can you make any suggestions for other sources? I only want the names of any books you know.

If it is more convenient to you we might meet in town on Monday or Tuesday evening, especially as I should have to run away early in the morning to put in an appearance at my Mother's.

    Yours ever
    E.T.

208

De la Mare wrote regularly for the quarterly Edinburgh Review *in 1913 and 1914 with the exception of October 1913. His April 1914 article covered eight books, including a review of Ralph Hodgson's 'Song of Honour' in one of the "richly embellished little chapbooks" for Fraser's publishing company, Flying Fame, and a rather cursory mention of Gibson, Brooke, Abercrombie and Drinkwater's* New Numbers. *De la Mare's next article was for the July 1914 edition, once again covering eight books.*

                                   Steep
                                   [postmarked 22 MR 14]

My dear de la Mare,

I was sorry to get your letter this morning because I can't now manage Tuesday & you can't Monday. But could you meet me outside Miles at 7 on <u>Wednesday</u>? I would stay till the 10.30 train that night if you could. Let me know at 13 Rusham Rd. Or would lunch that day suit you – anywhere at 1 or 1.30?

With love to you all & good luck with the Edinburgh article (which I never see)

    Yours ever
    E.T.

209

Steep
Wednesday

My dear de la Mare

This is to say I am very sorry indeed I did not see you & sorrier that I gave you such useless trouble. But when I suggested Wednesday I made sure I should hear by Tuesday night & did not think to tell you I was elsewhere that night. Your letter arrived <u>here</u> a few minutes after I did. I was uneasy but had no means of finding out, so I took an early train home, & was wretched at the sight of your letter forwarded from Balham. If you will send me just a word to say you are no longer irritated by my not turning up I shall be really pleased. I don't quite know when I can next come up. I am taking Mervyn & Bronwen to Wales about the 14th, & I suppose spending Easter Monday night in town. Shall you be at home? If so we might all come over in the afternoon, or I could come in the evening. Only, do not alter any plans because it is not perfectly certain Monday will be the day. Write a word or tell me I am as excusable as I feel. But I know I should be irritated & I at least have time to waste.

Yours ever
ET.

210

Steep
[in pencil, Before 12 April 1914]

My dear de la Mare

Thank you. Unless something quite unforeseen happens we shall be coming to town on or before Easter Monday & I at any rate will come over to you. I won't promise for the children because my mother would probably not want to part with them if they have only just arrived & are leaving next day: so I will let you know later. Don't forget, if any old books of exploration come into to your mind, to jot down the title for me. I suppose you don't possess Fowlis' edition of Hakluyt? Dent's in Everyman leaves me so much to do in identifying places.

I now appear to have been dropped by the Chronicle & taken on (at the end of a barge pole) by the Daily News. The fiction continues & I wonder how much less tedious it will be to read than it is to write, for it can't be more.

I wish you were coming down into Wales with us. We expect a week at Laugharne, where you never came in the flesh.

Yours ever

E.T.

211

Thomas was working on his autobiography The Childhood of Edward Thomas *in tandem with the "fiction" mentioned in the previous letter to de la Mare.*
The typist is Eleanor Farjeon.
Myfanwy frequently went to stay with John Freeman's family. They had a young daughter of their own.
There are no signed articles by de la Mare in the January to April 1914 issues of Times Literary Supplement *nor in the March and April issues of* Saturday Westminster Gazette.

STEEP,
PETERSFIELD.
29 April 1914

My dear de la Mare

Shall I send you the typescript of my autobiography up to abt 16, which is all but complete? It is a very bald thing in which I have not attempted to do more than record facts. No atmosphere, no explanation. Only the typist has read it & it is not a thing I want seen. In fact even should you think that when complete it might be published, I think I ought to omit my name & some other things that would help to show who the writer & people mentioned are.

My wife & I are going to have a holiday of a week or so beginning on the 22nd or thereabouts. The Freemans may have Baby & if we take her there on the Sunday (the 21st) we would like to come on to you. May we?

I liked the article on [dialect/Sickert?] in the Times. And — as I meant [to] have said at once — I liked your W.G. review. If ever anyone could be tempted to like that book it would be by your notice. Your quotations were the most persuasive possible. I almost liked the book myself that day.

My Proverbs wander round vainly seeking to be devoured.

Yours ever

E.T.

212

This undated letter is placed at the end of the Bodleian album. The reference to the M.S. and the Times *and* New Weekly *and the context of other letters to de la Mare suggest it was written in mid 1914.*

Steep

My dear de la Mare,

I am sorry I did not see you the week before last but I didn't know there was a chance of your coming to St George's. I am to be up tomorrow. If you are free at 1 or 4 anywhere in town send me a card

c/o Clifford Bax

House 'A'

Bishop's Avenue

East Finchley.

I am returning by an early train, & could make it 3.30 if you like.

I will send the M.S. soon. Without names I am almost certain it would only be recognizable to a very few.

The Times sends nothing. I asked for a book once or twice. The New Weekly is the only paper that does. So that things draw on more rapidly. As a rule I am really not much disturbed.

I don't know why Hooton should be ironical, unless to show he still could be.

We are now prevented from coming on the 21st (Sunday). I will let you know what day would be possible — a day or two later.

Ever yours

ET.

P.S. I forgot I shall be at St George's <u>tomorrow at</u> 3.30 in any case.

213

The Flowers I Love, an anthology of flower poems and drawings, was published by T.C. and E.C. Jacks in 1916. Thomas selected the poems. He included de la Mare's 'The Three Cherry Trees', 'The Child in the Story Awakes', 'The Hawthorn hath a deathly smell', 'A Widow's Weeds' and 'Ophelia'.
De la Mare and Frost eventually met in America in early 1917.

STEEP,
PETERSFIELD.
2 [or 9?] July 1914

My dear de la Mare,

I wanted to use 'The Child in the Story awakes' in my anthology, but I am not at all sure that Messrs Jack will pay £2.20 for it. I thought you would like to know what <u>Longmans</u> think the poems worth apiece.

You are probably in Cornwall, so don't trouble to answer this. I hope your weather suits.

If you are back on the 21st perhaps Frost will be in town & I should like you to meet him.

Yours ever
Edward Thomas

214

J.D. Beresford, writer, dramatist and journalist.

.

STEEP,
PETERSFIELD.
14 July   1914

My dear de la Mare,

I believe Jacks are going to pay the £2.20. I hope they will. – This is just to say I should really like to know what somebody else thought of the autobiography, & I do not mind whom you choose to try it on incognito. It would be well if I could see Beresford's opinion untempered. You see, I have a real fear that the thing was a mistake, & that I ensured leaving out everything by my method.

I hope I can see you before you go to Kent & we to Herefordshire (about the 4th of August). But I shall be back here on Wednesday or Thursday week just as you are returning home I suppose.

You don't happen to know anyone who would like to have this cottage for a month from about August 4 do you?

With our love,
Yours ever
E.T.

215

Thomas is staying with his family in Herefordshire for a month near Frost and his family. Harold Begbie was a prolific writer and journalist.

> c/o Mrs Chandler
> Ledington
> Ledbury
> Herefordshire
> [in pencil, = viii]
> 14 July 1914

My dear de la Mare   Thank you for the MS which came on to me here some days ago. One way & another we all got here by the 5th & are staying till the end of the month probably. I am sorry I shan't see you at Cowden this time. Ellis, I have heard, is looking for some job under the War department. I don't know what other poets are doing. It seems the day of Begbies. Poets might as well fight as write like Begbie or even like Bridges. How is trade with you? Is there any reviewing to be done at all? Neither editors nor anybody else writes to me. However, I shall have to be even idler than I am before I take up the Autobiography again. Yours ever
ET.

216

The poet and literary critic Lascelles Abercrombie.
Thomas reviewed Abercrombie's Speculative Dialogues *in the March 1914* Bookman.

The artist James Guthrie, whom Thomas met through Bottomley in early 1907, became a close friend, later illustrating and publishing some of Thomas's poems. When reviewing Guthrie's The Elf: A magazine of Drawing and Writing *in the January 1913* Bookman, *Thomas calls him "a poet who often emerges from his words as if peering out at us between them."*
The equilateral triangle refers to the Frosts, the Thomases and the de la Mares.

c/o Mrs Chandler
Ledington
Ledbury
Herefordshire
[in pencil, before 30 Aug '14]

My dear de la Mare

I am sorry I didn't acknowledge the M.S. before & then forgot the Cowden address. We are all here till early September. Mervyn & I cycled, taking three days thro Basingstoke Newbury Hungerford Swindon Cricklade Cirencester & Gloucester. My wife & the others had to motor at midnight from Malvern, the train turning them loose there & all lodgings full. This helped to put us or Frost or some mysterious connection under suspicion! We have had a good variety of mostly good weather. Being under half a mile from Frost's four children ours are provided for. We walk & cycle. I write what I can. But no publisher editor or public is concerned. The dribble of work has stopped. However I am lucky to have just finished that vile book I have been gnawing at a year now about writers & their native or chosen country. So I think we can hold out some time. But I know Abercrombie can't. He has connections who presumably won't let him & his two (shortly three) children starve, but if there is money to be given away he ought to be helped. I see him occasionally. I can't think of anyone else except Guthrie. He needs regular provision really: he has not enough luck or ingenuity.

I hope you are all right. People aren't going to let you be anything else so far as they can provide, though I expect you don't feel that it is so. — I stopped for 5 minutes thinking how I should justify this or make it plain. But I should only have other things to justify or make plain. Your wife & the children at any rate are all well I hope. Please give them our love We wish you were at the other corner of the triangle, & that an equilateral one.

Yours ever
E.T.

217

Austin Harrison, editor of English Review, *published Thomas's 'Tipperary' in October 1914, 'It's a Long, Long Way' in December 1914, and 'This England' in April 1915. Thomas also wrote a similar article 'Soldiers Everywhere' for* The New Statesman, *published in 8 May 1915.*

De la Mare frequently published poems in the Saturday Westminster Gazette. *Recent ones included 'Mrs Grundy' on 21 March 1914, and 'The Exile' on 25 April 1914, both later published in* Motley and Other Poems, *1918. 'I went to pluck a flow'r' appeared on 18 May, 'To A Child' on 23 May, and 'A True-Blue Broadside of '14' on 22 August 1914, all uncollected.*

De la Mare's poem 'Happy England' in the 27 August 1914 Times Literary Supplement *and* Motley and Other Poems, *1918, is criticized as "patriotic" by Virginia Woolf in her 18 October 1917* Times Literary Supplement *review of* Motley.

BLAST *was the short-lived literary magazine of the Vorticist movement. It was edited by Wyndham Lewis, with Ezra Pound as its main publicist. The first issue on 2 July 1914 included contributions from Pound; the sculptors Henri Gaudier-Brzeska (later killed at Verdun) and Jacob Epstein; the Camden Town Group painter Spencer Gore; the artist Edward Walsworth; and the writer, journalist and literary critic Rebecca West. It also contained an extract from what later became Ford Madox Ford's* The Good Solider.

c/o Mrs Chandler
Ledington
Ledbury
Herefordshire
30 August 1914

My dear de la Mare,

I have left a letter of yours unnoticed. There was not much to say. I tried Richmond with an article but not military, not even anti-military. He returned it. Now I have a poor difficult job for Austin Harrison which takes me over the Midlands & North for the next week or two. Then I shall be back & shall see you. Meantime I have only heard of your 2 poems (Times & W.G). I wish I had seen them. Hodgson is guarding Chelsea Gas Works. Rupert Brooke I hear has joined the army. The Blast poets I hear have not. If the war goes on I believe I shall find myself a sort of Englishman, tho neither poet nor soldier. If I could earn anything worthwhile as a soldier I think I should go.

Florence was ill when you wrote. I hope she is well again & all

of you the better for August – we never had a better month.
> Yours ever
> E.T.

218

De la Mare's regular contribution to the Edinburgh Review *ceased in October 1914.*
Thomas's P.S. is written in pencil.

> 13 Rusham Road
> Thursday

My dear de la Mare. I am sorry you can't come, because I have to go home this afternoon to write about my travels (for the English Review — my last job apparently) which will take me some days & it has to appear on Oct. 1. I don't know quite when I shall be up again. There is no business to allege as a reason & I imagine that I am going to dig in the garden & save minor expenses, while considering whether I can in reason & decency enlist. I wish they would conscribe me & settle my hesitations. At this moment things seem improving, but to be away perhaps 3 years out of action as far as wage-earning goes might be for everyone's good but I don't really like the idea.

I hope you still have the Times & Edinburgh & to some extent the Westminster. The question is what to do with spare time. It is not easy – if possible – to go on writing as if the County Council ran the world: otherwise it would be a good time for doing what one really wants to do, provided one can really discover now what that is. Perhaps you haven't the same trouble. I hope not. I am sure you have a better idea of England than I have.

When I do come up again I will let you know.
> Yours ever
> ET.

P.S. Forgive me for forgetting, at the time that you are not in town as a matter of course.

219

Edward Garnett served as a civilian ambulance orderly during the war.

13 Rusham Rd.
Balham
29 September 1914

My dear de la Mare

I met Garnett today & I should think from the way he spoke that he would not mind having one of the posts you spoke of, if they ever exist. If the list is not too full, will you mention him?

Yours ever
ET.

220

Harry Hooton was a one-time banking colleague of de la Mare's.

Steep
Petersfield
1 October 1914

My dear de la Mare

Though I am afraid of tiring you with asking I want to ask you if Guthrie's name can be put down as one needing keep at this time. He has been here for a day or two & I gather that he is really hit & worse off than he has been. Also I believe that one of his less irregular sources of supply has dried up for other reasons. [Deleted sentence]. I cross out an unnecessary obvious remark.

Did you see a reference to Balfour & some such scheme as you told me of in one of the Sunday papers? I was told of it but did not see it or learn precisely what was said. It would be nice to see you more often this winter.

Hooton by the way is safe & comfortable at present — seated however on the grave of his business, it appears, tho there is a chance of exhuming it after the war. He is making sloe gin as in other years.

Yours ever
ET.

221

Thomas's 'It's a long, long way' appeared in the December 1914 English Review.
New Numbers *volume 1-4, a publication of the Dymock poets (Wilfrid Wilson Gibson, Rupert Brooke, Lascelles Abercrombie and John Drinkwater) came out between February and December 1914. De la Mare reviews Gibson's* Borderlands: Thoroughfares *in the 15 October* Times Literary Supplement. *In reference to ghosts, de la Mare reports that "Mr Gibson has not definitely proved he is at home in all these parts,. But poem after poem shows how much he is inclined to trespass there." He is "not convincing. […] There is too often the touch of exaggeration that only blurs and spoils the impressions", and every "epithet there has some truth in it but it is a truth beneath at least three coats of conventional paint."*
Thomas's mention of Gibson in his November 1914 Bookman *article 'John Masefield and Wilfrid Gibson', is lukewarm and pointedly brief, the bulk of the review being devoted to Masefield.*

Steep
Petersfield
16 October 1914

My dear de la Mare,

I heard from Guthrie by the same post. Thank you very much for what you have done for him. I hope to see you before the end of the month & hear what you have to say about Zeppelins & c, but I hear almost nothing. I have been journeying in Wales & the border & am this moment in Herefordshire on my way home. Of course very little work turns up but I am doing another article for the 'English Review' & one way & another I have enjoyed the Autumn more than a patriot ought to, no doubt, tho I <u>imagine</u> I could have enjoyed work too. I hope you have had plenty. I thought I saw your hand in a just & considerate review of W.W. Gibson's efforts yesterday. We agree perfectly there.

> Love to you all
> Yours ever
> Edward Thomas

222

This undated note is placed at the end of the Bodleian album, but the context of the surrounding notes help place it here.

Steep
Thursday

My dear de la Mare,

Thank you. I will come on Monday But May I come in time for lunch & leave you at 6? I had just written saying I would come in the evening & stay till after breakfast when a letter came from Hooton (from Somerset) saying they won't be home till that evening which is my last available one. I hope you are free as you say 'any time', but I could come on Sunday evening & stay that night if it suited you. Unless I hear (at 13 Rusham Rd) I will come before 1 on Monday.

Yours ever
E.T.

223

~~Steep~~
13 Rusham Rd
Balham SW.
31 October 1914

~~I am very glad. I will come to supper on Monday &~~ ~~breakfast on Tuesday. But I will come as early as I can after lunch or even to lunch if I come straight from the Hootons. I have not heard from them, though, & perhaps they are away.~~
If you are in town on Tuesday will you come to the Mt Blanc in Gerrard St at 1.30 or St George's at 4. If not,   E.T.
what about lunch on Thursday?

224

[postmarked 2 NO 14]

I am coming up a day earlier so I have Tuesday evening free. Can
you meet me in town or shall I come to you? Send me a card
tonight at 13 Rusham Rd if you are free.

E.T.
Monday

225

31 Rusham Road
Balham SW
Sunday
[postmarked 16 NOV [?]4]

Dear Mrs de la Mare

Thank you very much for letting me know. I am glad it is over,
but of course you will have the worst yet now till Jack is well again.
I can't imagine writing anything to him but I wonder could I see
him perhaps on Wednesday? If you do happen to know when I
could will you send me a word at

1 Bishop's Avenue, East Finchley?
Helen is at Chiswick now for some days. in case you don't know
the address it is 14 Duke's Avenue, Chiswick W.

With love to the children all but especially jenny lucy Yours ever

Edward Thomas

226

Clifford Bax lived at 1 Bishop's Avenue.

On Wednesday night I shall be
at 1 Bishop's Avenue East Finchley NW.   13 Rusham Rd
                                                      Tuesday

My dear de la Mare,

I do hope the enemy in your midst is really disarmed now. I will certainly come & see you & the beard. Probably I shall be returning from Clapham Junction on Thursday 7 so I will come to tea with you at 4 unless meantime you make some other proposal (after getting my 2nd card). Is there anything I can do or bring with me?

Seccombe came over unexpectedly last week to get away from German prisoners for a time. He was very well, trying to prove that he was upset to inarticulateness by the war at the same time that he was writing & lecturing continuously. He was telling the story about English Tommies burying German dead & coming across a half-corpse which said 'I am not yet dead' & covering him up with the remark that 'You can't believe a word they say.'

> Yours ever
> E.T.

227

De la Mare was in hospital with appendicitis.

> 1 Bishop's Avenue
> East Finchley
> 18 November 1914

Dear Mrs de la Mare

I sat with Jack for an hour this morning & hope he found it no longer than I did. He did not seem to. He was practically his complete old self, but without the physical energy of expression to accompany his thoughts. Also he spoke of being mostly comfortable and at rest. So that I should really expect him to be the better for it. Perhaps it will all count mainly as rest. I enjoyed being there with him. I even liked the view (it was misted) from that window. If I can I shall go again tomorrow before getting home. I hope soon to hear that you two are better. Did he show you his oriental potentate with pearl head dress drawn on a sheet of the 'Times'?

> Yours ever
> Edward Thomas

228

Edward Marsh edited the five Georgian anthologies published between 1912 and 1922.

                                            Steep
                                            Petersfield
                                            30 November 1914

My dear de la Mare,

   I am sorry I didn't come again to see you but I hear you had
troops of visitors & perhaps too many. The time went quickly that
Wednesday & I hope I didn't stay too long. I shall be up next week
& should like to know where I could see you & what would be the
best time. That will be better than a letter. But there is one thing I
meant to mention before & that is, that I gather Marsh is not
including Ellis or Frost in his 2nd Georgian Poetry. Do you think
he knows their work? I think they would make the book more
interesting & representative than if it is a repetition of the first plus
Hodgson only, & I wonder if you feel able to mention them to
Marsh. He is probably not friendly to me or my opinion or I would
write direct. He ought to see 'Mowing' or 'The Tuft of Heaven' in
Frost's first book, 'A Boy's Will' (Nutt 1913).

   If you can write now, send me a word or at least an oriental
profile & a thousand pearls. With our love to you both
                                    Yours ever
                                    E.T.

                                    229

De la Mare was convalescing at Harrington Gardens.
Thomas wrote of the second Georgian anthology to Frost on 6 December 1915
that "I had a faint chance of getting in" and that the "only things I really much
like are de la Mare's and perhaps Davies's. Bottomley maybe alright."
De la Mare appeared in all the Georgian anthologies, Thomas in none.

                                            Steep
                                            Monday
                                            [postmarked ? DE]
                                            [in pencil, 7 Dec ?14]

I think I can manage <u>Thursday</u> at 4 & hope to find Harrington
Gardens. I have an idea that Georgian Poetry II is coming out in
the Spring. So I thought Frost might still be introduced. I hear that
Ezra Pound was invited to the first so being an American is no bar.
                                            E.T.

230

Esmé Wingfield-Stratford's The History of British Patriotism *was published in 1913.*
Thomas composed his first mature poem 'Up in the Wind' on 3 December and had already written nine more by the middle of the month. One of them, 'Interval', carries echoes of verses of de la Mare's 'Alone' ["No sound over the deep"], which Thomas quoted in both February 1909 and December 1910 in the English Review, *and also of 'Mrs MacQueen' in* Peacock Pie.

Steep
18 December 1914

My dear de la Mare,

Can you lend me Esmé Wingfield-Stratford's 'Patriotism' from your own shelves or the London Library? Lane published it you may remember a year or 2 back & I want to see if it leaves me anything to do in a similar direction. Will you? tho I have a feeling that I made you shy by returning your 'Lyly' spattered with ink — I don't know by whom.

Will you be in on Monday afternoon, because if you are I might come in on my way to Hooton's? But it's uncertain, depends on whether I can ride to London on Sunday or see a chance of doing so on Monday — if I rode on Monday I couldn't come to you. Send me a card to say if you are free & I can probably let you know by Monday whether to expect me. I hope you are getting on and not writing too many verses.   Yours ever

E.T.

231

In April 1915 the English Review *published Thomas's essay, 'This England'. Several images from it resurface in his May 1916 poem 'The sun used to shine'.*

Steep
31 December 1914

My dear de la Mare,

I was very glad to get Wingfield Stratford's book, or vol. I of it, this morning. I am sending you the enclosed in case you can ask them to send vol. II here when it is ready. I am trying to get an idea of how the sentiment of England has grown. An article for the English Review is the immediate purpose. It is all I have to do.

I hope you are getting well & liking being well again. Are any of your new verses visible now?

The year is just ending & we have to sing Auld Lang Syne with a houseful of sleepy children. Our best wishes to you all.

Yours ever
E.T.

232

De la Mare's convalescence resulted in a run of creativity, scribbling rhymes for a book to be illustrated by Ralph Hodgson. "He goes on all day, covering sheets of paper with that small weird writing", writes Henry Newbolt to Alice Hylton on 20 January 1915. The book never materializes.

Thomas has a similar creative surge. Between December and early February he writes thirty three poems, finishing 'House and Man' on 4 February.

In This England: an anthology from her writers, *published in 1915, Thomas included under the pseudonym Edward Eastaway two of his own poems: 'Haymaking' and 'The Manor Farm'. He also includes de la Mare's 'Trees' and 'The Echoing Green'. The anthology includes work by all the names listed in this letter apart from Gray.*

De la Mare completed his long poem, 'Cathay', the saga of a King and his Queen Oo-Chee, at about this time.

Steep
4 February 1915

My dear de la Mare,

I heard you were away or I would have seen you last week. I hope you really are better & didn't find the rest a weariness altogether, as unfortunately I know it can be. For I got a sprained ankle with the new year which kept me in 3 weeks & looks now as if I ought to have let it keep me in six. This may keep me from town for a time. When I am up I shall see you. It was an exaggerated form of the truth you heard. Mervyn is going out to New Hampshire with the Frosts on Saturday week. My following him is uncertain. I seldom feel like the experiment, or any experiment or I shouldn't be here now. We have got Bronwen home again now.

The 2nd vol. of Patriotism didn't arrive. The first is turning out useful for an anthology I am at for the Oxford Press — an <u>English</u>

anthology of the most English prose & verse I can get, English character, landscape & thought. Chaucer, Shakespeare, Milton, Wordsworth, Gray, Latimer, Bunyan, Cobbett, Johnson, Borrow & c. Tell me at least one thing to put in. Of course it is being done at top speed. It is about all I have to do, or I shouldn't think so much about going to America.

Is your long poem fit for the human eye (of E.T.)? I hope you are not getting the usual doses of cold. We have had a house almost full of it, & my wife & baby are quite poorly now. I thought of you over at Netherhampton while I was abed here, & wished we could share some of your rest. Yours ever

E.T.

233

As well as de la Mare's 'Trees' and 'The Echoing Green', This England includes poems by Thomas Hardy, C.M. Doughty, Gordon Bottomley, and a prose extract from W.H. Hudson.

Steep
22 February 1915

My dear de la Mare, I want to put one of your poems in my anthology, tho I am probably not taking any other living poet's work, unless Doughty turns lenient. Can you give me leave, & can you recommend me anyone that you think specially suitable in a very English anthology? 'Trees' is one of the most suitable. 'John Mouldy' occurs to me: also the Lady of the West Country. I may be sending in the M.S. at the end of this week, so if you do recommend anything let it be soon. I hope Colin is better & you yourself better than when I saw you.

Yours ever
E.T.

234

In the 4 June 1912 Daily Chronicle, Thomas describes C.M. Doughty's 'The Cliffs' as "a poem of extraordinary dignity, fervour and sweetness, including fairy scenes unequalled outside 'A Midsummer Night's Dream'." Doughty's

'Wild England', 'The Elves's Wedding', 'Grey Deep' and 'An Englishman in Arabia' are included in This England.

Thomas's later June 1916 Bookman *review of Doughty's* The Titans *calls him "the prophet-priest, among English poets" and celebrates his "epic tenderness". He laments that this book "must wait till the England he so reverences returns, or, if it has not disappeared, awakes to consciousness. His is a solitary voice, clear as a trumpet, but very distant." Thomas's own poem, 'The Trumpet', in which the trumpet call "chases the dreams of men" urging them to wake to consciousness, was written at the end of September 1916.*

Thomas's 'Thomas Hardy of Dorchester' appeared in the June 1913 Poetry and Drama, *and was revised for his* In Pursuit of Spring *in 1914. Thomas notices "in his [Hardy's] poetry something which I hope I may with respect call rustic, and, what is much the same thing, old-fashioned" and observes "how often is he delighted to present a peasant's view, a peasant's contribution to the irony of things".*

Steep

My dear de la Mare,

Thank you, & Doughty is coming in after all. Would you mind if I took 'Trees' (or/and) the 'Epitaph'? Then I think I will. I wish you could put me on to the right things in Doughty. I have got 2pp. of the fairy's wedding ('Cliffs') & a short bit about the 'grey deep' & a longer about the journey of the deity & the sacred waggon, from 'The Dawn in Britain.' There was a passage in 'Arabia Deserta' too that I cannot find, when he says he wouldn't pretend to be a Mahometan to save his life but might have pretended a legend Confucius or Buddha (or Socrates) as prophets.

I am all right except that I badly want to walk about a bit. Sitting down here all day long wouldn't be the sort of fun I prefer in any case. I make it the worse probably by smoking a lot of the time.

Ellis looked better I thought. But he has rounded out since he took to motoring. He has no exercise at all & doesn't object at all either, especially as his heart's weak.

Poor Dick. Is he lying abed looking at snow? We have quite a pretty inch or two on the hills, though here it is turned to mud.

There were things I could, should have taken from Hardy. But I heard he was annoyed by my article in 'Poetry & Drama.' (I said he was a peasant) & I daren't ask now.   Yours ever

E.T.

235

A favourite pupil of William Johnson Cory, poet and educator, was de la Mare's influential teacher at St Paul's, Canon Henry Scott-Holland. Ella Coltman, Margaret Newbolt and Mary Coleridge also studied Greek with Cory.

Steep
25 February 1915

My dear de la Mare, I am sorry you are troubling about the book. It doesn't matter a bit. I have just done without it, & as I have to avoid most copyright work it is just as well. But I wonder would you send Constable's a word? They would be less likely to charge me 2/6 a line which they wanted to for Meredith, but I declined. I wish you had mentioned the scene of 'There live but three good men unhanged.' Now I want it I can't find it & the idiotic Concordance has no reference to 'unhanged.' I have not looked at Cory just as I haven't looked at any recent writers I did not know well. The old or the unquestionable are the best for my purpose, the difficulty being to avoid the obvious & yet be sound. I can't bring myself to include Gray's Elegy & yet it & 'John Gilpin' & 'When icicles hang by the wall' & the 'Canterbury Tales' are the most English things there are. I am omitting Gilpin too.

It was Garnett told me about Hardy. He had it from Scott-James who had been visiting Hardy. It is a pity because I have a very great admiration for Hardy's poetry & some rustic parts of his novels.   Yours ever
E.T.

236

Thomas had composed 44 poems by the date of this letter.

Steep
21 March 1915

My dear de la Mare,

You never told me if you had mentioned 'Epitaph' & 'Trees' to Constable. Is it all right? I think the Oxford Press will pay a reasonable fee, as it is the only one I have incurred.

I am sending you some verses by a very young poet (not a young man) who desires to remain anonymous except to you & one or two other people. Don't mention them anywhere, as they are to be published (if at all) under a pseudonym. He is coming to town next week & hopes to see you & remains

Yours ever

E.T.

whatever (in reason) you think of the young poet.

237

Thomas was using the pseudonym Edward Eastaway for his poetry.
De la Mare took on the Royal Society of Literature Chair of Fiction in March
1915. He was also awarded a Civil List Pension of £100 a year for life

Steep

24 March 1915

My dear de la Mare,

The young poet must be much vainer or more tricky than you are used to. He can't imagine how he will stand waiting a week or how then he could stand hearing he has gone wrong over metre sometimes & yet (apparently) not always. But he does think you may be right because he agrees with you in liking those 4.* He wishes you could prepare him for the horrible truth (it must be horrible) beforehand. Keep the verses till then by all means.

And then your own news withheld is perhaps more tantalising. Are you free on Tuesday evening, or on Wednesday either for lunch or supper? Or tea on Tuesday? Send me a card soon to say which suits or what other time suits, for I might be still up on Thursday.

Thank you for getting at Constable's.

The Proverbs seem dead but still can't find a publisher to pay funeral expenses, & I believe nearly all London publishers have been invited. They prefer Belgians as objects of charity, so that if I can get my ankle really mended I shall have to try to serve my country after all. The gardener next door has just been called up & when I heard him talking about it I felt worse than I have done yet.

Yours ever

E.T.

P.S. I expect I did ask you not to mention the verses to anyone &
told you I was sending them about under another na[me]

* But then the poor fellow likes the others too.

238

Thomas was writing The Life of the Duke of Marlborough *for Chapman
and Hall.*

(I am now at <u>13 Rusham Rd</u>)   Steep
Monday
[in pencil, 1915]

My dear de la Mare,

Yours is the only interesting criticism I've had. But I think it is
probably too fundamental, considering that I wrote (if anything)
with a feeling that I did use the Morse code. This is a fact. I only
hope someone beside myself will catch the accent. They all seemed
speakable tho none chantable. However I can see you soon now. I
have to come up tomorrow. Is there any lunch or tea time we could
meet –Wednesday Thursday or Friday? It is work I have come for
& I am not sure I shall not have to work in the evenings. But if you
are not in town any of those days I will come to you, which in any
case I should have liked to do – but the work is pressing, & too
uncongenial to be left hanging about. 'So no more now.'

Yours ever
E.T.

Yes do send the poems when they are ready.
And by the way can you lend me Coxe's 'Memoirs of the Duke
of Marlborough' from the L.L.? I will meet you at the L.L. if
necessary.

239

Thomas was thinking of going to America to join Frost.

Steep
Petersfield.
2 June 1915

My dear de la Mare,

Thank you for all you say. At present my anxiety is for the day after tomorrow so I don't need anything but a prospect. They tell me I have very little chance of a pension & I know I have less chance of anything else so I rather expect I shall disappear early in September unless it is as well to go before. You can imagine I don't like it & you may not be able to imagine how little I dare to hope from it. So August is very uncertain. I expect I shall sit rather tight at home. But if I travel I should like to find you at the other end. Next week however I think we can meet. Is Tuesday night possible? If not, send me a card & say if either Wednesday or Thursday will do. One of those days I shall be booked, but I am not yet sure which. Our love to all of you

Yours ever

E. Thomas

240

Thomas is staying at the house of solicitor and amateur botanist J.W. Haines on a cycling trip. They visit May Hill where he begins composing 'Words', noting on the manuscript "Hucclecote – on the road from Gloster to Coventry", 26-28 June 1915.

HILLVIEW ROAD,
HUCCLECOTE, GLOS.
Saturday
[in pencil, 26 June 1915]

My dear de la Mare

I was almost sorry to run into you by chance last week because I should have arranged to see you, but it was an unexpected visit. The week after next I shall be up again & see you. At the moment I am travelling to work off the effects of writing a book on Marlborough, which looks like my last job here. So I am planning to go to America in a month or 2 to see if there is anything to be had there.

You feel a little safer with your pension I hope. There is to be an attempt to get one for me but they say I have a very poor chance in a crowd of more elderly & more celebrated applicants.

I am at Gloster for a day with an admirer of yours who has just taken me to Painswick to see a house that reminds him of you. But there were 100 other houses you would like there, all stately stone however small, & all with great views from the hillside over the Cotswolds. It is the place with 100 years in the churchyard where no one can count beyond 99. I am now going N E through Stratford to Coventry & back home by Oxford. How poor freedom is when it is thrown at you.

Yours ever
E.T.

241

Steep
Petersfield
Sunday

Many thanks. I will come as early as I can on Tuesday but I must get back to Balham at midnight.

E.T.

242

13 Rusham Rd
Balham SW.
[postmarked 14 JUL 15]

If you are thereabouts will you come into St George's before 6 tomorrow? In case you are to be in town on Thursday at lunch time send a word here & I will let you know for certain by Thursday morning whether I can meet you — say at [Miles?] at 1.

E.T.

243

Thomas enlists in the Artist's Rifles in mid July 1915.

13 Rusham Rd
Balham
28 July 1915

I am afraid there is no chance of my coming over this week, but could you meet me on Saturday at Miles's at 1.30? I am going home afterwards. Or I usually lunch at the Lyons' (smoking room at back) near the top of Tottenham Court Rd on the <u>left</u>. I get there at 1 & have an hour, & will look for your tomorrow (when I shall probably have over an hour) and Friday in case you happen to be up.

P.S.   E.T.

If you were free on Tuesday evening next week I think I could come to you.

244

Thomas composed eleven poems in July and in August was correcting proofs of Four-and-Twenty Blackbirds *and indexing his book on Marlborough.*

13 Rusham Rd
Balham SW.
28 August 1915

My dear de la Mare,

This is only to say I am sorry I have not been able to come down. Until now my weekends (of 24 hours) I have spent at home. The 24 hours now before me I could have spent with you. But it would have been mostly railway journey, getting back late on Sunday night, & I want a rest. In fact even going home was more a habit than anything else. So I am staying on here tonight & going to be picked up by Hooton's car for a day's ride. This is now my 4th full week of drill. I have enjoyed it all as much as I could without liking any of the people or rather without getting on with any of them at all. We are expecting to be in town some time longer because the camp is unfinished or not ready for a whole new company of 250. If you are back then next week or the week after I may still see you, I hope. Let me know, so that I can arrange it. I see Ellis & the 2 Freemans sometimes but I mostly prefer to be idle in my evenings with a glance at 'Infantry Training 1914'. My foot is all right & I begin dimly to look forward to something different.

With love to you all
Yours ever
E.T.

245

A few Bookman *reviews by Thomas continue to be published: on William Morris in June 1915, on Blake in August 1915, on C.M. Doughty in June 1916 and on W.H. Davies in August 1916.*

13 Rusham Rd
Balham SW
31 August 1915

My dear de la Mare

I couldn't come next week end. My wife is coming up for a day or two with Baby & Bronwen. But my letter will tell you it really wasn't possible anyhow. As for reviewing, it is almost as well there is none left for me. I couldn't do it. I had one left over when I joined & it will have to wait till the war is over. Then of course I shall have to find a 3rd trade, if the difficulty isn't otherwise solved. But I don't think much about it & never dismally. — I shall see you then I hope towards the end of next week either at Anerley or up in town. You seem to have liked it better than you expected. I hope the children have done too. There has been a fortnight of the best weather in town, thrown away on drill of course. We shall not go to camp this week or next, most likely. When we do perhaps a cake would find a good home there. Thank you for the idea. My love to all of you, without telling you what I should most like to see in Oxford unless it is one or two chestnut trees looking over into the street from behind high old walls. Perhaps you saw them.

Yours ever
E.T.

246

13 Rusham Rd
Balham.
[postmarked 10 SEP 15]

I feel sure my wife has written & I suppose it must have been to Anerley, so that you will know now when to expect her. I had thought of coming over, if there was room for any more Thomas, on Saturday evening or Sunday. Saturday evening perhaps would

be better as Helen & Baby will be arriving then from town & I
could come with them.

> E.T.

247

> 13 Rusham Rd
> [postmarked 17 SEP 15]

I was quite unexpectedly warned on Tuesday that I was to go to
camp on Friday & since then I have had no time. This address is
safest for the present till I know my Company. Perhaps I shall be
able to get to you some Saturday or Sunday before long.

> E.T.

248

> Pte. P. E. Thomas
> 5 Platoon
> B Company
> Artists Rifles
> High Beech, nr Laughton,
> Essex.
> Tuesday
> [postmarked 28 SP 15]

My dear de la Mare

There isn't any news except that I have been enjoying the
country & the fine weather & the hard work in spite of the rough
conditions. One isn't inclined to write much & not encouraged by
the noisy crowded scanty rooms. Nor can I get away except every
other Saturday night, & then I must see either my people or my
wife. But when I have a Saturday night with my people I hope I
can get over to you.   Yours ever
> [E T]

249

> High Beech
> [postmarked 21 OC 15]

This is only to say all is uncertain here, but as we expect to leave for London (13 Rusham Rd for me) on Saturday don't write here till I can tell you something certain. If I do get to town on Saturday I am aiming at ~~getting to~~ having lunch at St George's at 1 or 1.30 & tea at 4.30.   E.T.

<h3 style="text-align:center">250</h3>

This pencilled letter is undated and placed at the end of the Bodleian album. However, the reference to cake, camp and arrangements to meet all suggest the date of October 1915.

My dear de la Mare,

It so happens I could manage Sunday afternoon, I shall be at Rusham Rd till after dinner & come over to you by 3 or soon after. The worst of it is I must be at Liverpool St at 8.30 to get into camp in time. But we can have a talk – so I need not write more – except to thank you for the idea of a cake, which is a very good one. We are really at work at last, thank goodness. I hope your wife will be better by Sunday. Send a word to 13 Rusham Rd if the time isn't convenient, will you?

Yours ever
E.T.

<h3 style="text-align:center">251</h3>

On 17 October, Thomas sends Eleanor Farjeon his first poem for two months, composed on 15-16 October, entitled 'October'.

A Coy
Artists Rifles
Suntrap
Laughton
Essex
[in pencil, [Oct] 1915]

My dear de la Mare,

Unless you can get over here some Sunday I am afraid it might be some time before we can meet. It is very hard to get away. But I will try to manage it in a fortnight's time. If you do come on Sunday week say (Sunday I hope to be home) I must tell you I am not allowed out of rather narrow bounds in the forest, but could meet you at the Robin Hood, 1 mile from Laughton Station on the road here. That is the best you can do. If you can't, send me a cake any time you like <u>after</u> next Sunday. Not Herbert Spencer I can read nothing, not even a paper: only 'Company Training'. Nor write. I have had one or 2 books offered me for review but it is utterly impossible. I don't think about books or writing except on a sleepless night when I sometimes make a few lines <u>and a half</u> & don't bother to write them down. Otherwise I should want to see Forest Reid on Yeats. It <u>is</u> a little like fashion of 1914, or like London when one is in the country content. I look forward to comparing notes with Dick & I shouldn't be surprised if he knows more than I do. This week, & I know not how much longer, I am digging clay & carting it in a barrow – the hardest work I ever did. But the weather is fine.

My love to you all
      Yours ever
            E.T

252

13 Rusham Rd
[postmarked 27 OCT 15]

I have been sent back here. Your letter greeted me on the first & last night of my return to High Beech. I will see you next week, but could you come to St George's tomorrow at 5.

E.T.

253

13 Rusham Rd.
[postmarked 2 NOV 15]

I will come on Wednesday as soon as I can.   E.T.

254

Added to the letter is the pencilled date of 'Sept? 1915' but the mention of the cake and the context of surrounding letters suggest it was written in October.

> 5 Platoon
> B Co
> Artists Rifles
> High Beech
> Laughton Essex
> Friday

My dear de la Mare,

Posts go very wrong here but your cake arrived on Wednesday, your letter only the next day. I was very glad of both though the evenings were too busy for me to write till now. We have had lectures & night operations every evening. The Zeppelin raid interrupted a lecture on Wednesday night. We saw one Zeppelin like a salmon tilted up in the search light. It must have got very near you by accounts I have heard. I hope it didn't give you even a sleepless night.

The cakes were & their remains still are very good. They help our plain midday bread & cheese or bread & sausage, out admirably. Yesterday all day we were at a trench in perfect hot weather & 3 people were much the better for your cakes. The beauty I see in short intervals here is becoming quite a compensation; all the more so because one never goes out to do anything but work. 'They' are farther off than ever though. And after all I count the days to get to a week's end. The air is full of rumours of an early move of camp, but I shall try to get away for Saturday night next week. Could you meet me in town for lunch if I do manage it? On the other hand I have injured my knee & might be given a couple of days off for it tomorrow & if so I will suggest an earlier meeting. I will let you know immediately. I am sorry to hear the surgeon hasn't done so much better than the creator with your innards. Or is it that 'they' are too strong?

> Yours ever

255

Written in pencil.
De la Mare was giving a series of lectures at the London Library Reading Room. The beginning of 'Home' ("Fair was the morning") composed on 7 and 10 March 1916 reflects the landscape Thomas alludes to here.
The 23 October 1915 Saturday Westminster Gazette *notice reads in full* "Mr. Edward Thomas makes a timely appeal with 'The Life of the Duke of

*Marlborough' (Chapman and Hall, 10s. 6d net), in which the story of the
campaigns of the great General and the political history of Marlborough's time
are combined with an independent study of his career and character." However,
Walter Sichel reviewed it at length in the 4 November 1915* Times Literary
Supplement, *writing that "Mr Thomas has written not only a very brilliant
and concentrated account of Marlborough, but one in which the whole man
[…] breathes and moves and has his being."*
*De la Mare's description of Hodgson's writing in a review of his poems in the
7 October 1915* Times Literary Supplement *gives a picture of the man: "his
speech is as clean and incisive as a blow", praising his work as "bare, vivid,
wasteless – as near action as words can be".*

> 4229 Hut 35
> Artists Rifles
> Harehall Camp
> nr Romford
> 24 November 1915

My dear de la Mare,

I couldn't get to your lecture, though the ticket came in good
time to remind me. I should like to have heard you & had a look at
Hodgson – I hear he was there. And now I have been 10 days in a
new camp, a very comfortable one on a nasty low flat piece of land
near Gidea Park Station. Except for some interesting men in my
new department I haven't enjoyed it much. We have been at a loose
end which is not the same thing as being free, & I have had a
cough into the bargain. However, we have discovered some
country that looked beautiful under the snow, & have explored it
rather thoroughly in making a contoured map of it. For some time
we expected to return to town to work, & we are still not without
hopes. It is so much easier to persuade company Commanders to
send their man to us in town than it is here. Not to speak of the
fact that we can see friends & get every week end in town. I don't
know when or for how long I shall get off next & fear it may be
some time before I get to Anerley again.

I hear there was a review of my Marlborough in the W.G. &
wonder if you did it? I see very few reviews of all my books. Did I
tell you I was made a lance corporal a week or two back? Love to
you all.   E. T.

256

Written in pencil.

4229
A. Company, Artists
Harehall Camp
nr Romford
30 November
[postmarked 1 DE 15]

My dear de la Mare,

In the Summer Garnett said he intended to try to get me something on the Civil List. He wasn't very hopeful & I think he can't have done any thing. Is it too late now? Do you think all the likely applications are in? I heard that somebody was having his pension doubled & thought perhaps I had a chance. No chance of getting to Anerley yet. Ever yours E. T.

257

Written in pencil.

4229
A. Company
Hare Hall Camp
Romsford
Saturday
[in pencil, Before Christmas 1915]

My dear de la Mare,

Hudson is ill in hospital in Cornwall, but writes a long letter to say that Garnett once mentioned the subject & that is all. He himself has done nothing & did not know he was expected to do anything. So he says. Let me know what has been done, if anything, & I will do what I can as soon as I can. It may be some time, a week or two or more. I replied that I would speak to you & told him I assumed that would not interfere with whatever he did. I only hope it is not too late. I am thinking chiefly of Mervyn. If I am to do much for him in the next year or two I must have more than I can probably or conceivably earn.

We have had no announcements about Xmas leave, but if we get several days I hope I can see you in town on my way home or back, if not at Anerley.

> Yours ever
> Edward Thomas

258

Written in pencil.

> Hare Hall Camp
> 13 December 1915

My dear de la Mare,

Thank you. I don't think anything will be gained by waiting for Hudson. He may not be able to do anything for some time. Whether he was hopeful or not I can't say. He didn't express a shade of opinion. Personally I can't see that 2 or 3 years should make any difference, unless of course it was a competition, with marks for age, deserts, degree of indigence & c. Upon my soul, I don't care a damn whether anything comes of it or not.

I will let you know about Christmas. But of course some people will have to stay behind & I might be one.

> Yours ever
> E.T.

259

Written in pencil.
During the illness referred to here Thomas produced several poems, including the ruminative pieces about familial and intimate love: 'I may come near to loving you', 'Those things that poets said' and 'No one so much as you'.

> 13 Rusham Rd
> Balham
> 7 February 1915
> [in pencil [16]]

My dear de la Mare,

I was disappointed by your letter but as it fell out I couldn't have come on Sunday. I developed a chill & here I am absent without leave till I can go out & return to camp. If you had been at home you might have come to see me. It is most deadly lying down unable to read or write or even to doze – it may be some time again before I have more than an hour or 2 in town. I think I told you I had less freedom now. Also I am in D. Company's black books. They refused me my 2nd stripe a fortnight ago because I had reported a man present who didn't turn up till next morning. This made me very sick. But for it I should have been a sergeant by the Spring. To wear bayonet on my hip was the height of my ambition. Well this is all the news except that my full address is

    L/Cpl P E Thomas 4229
        D Coy   Artists Rifles OTC
          Hut 15
            Hare Hall Camp
              Romford

I quite expect to be back there on Thursday as the chill seems to have begun to mend.

Oh, Ellis called at 5 yesterday to take me over there to dine. He had just called for you & found you out.

Well, I wish I had just set out from Salisbury past Netherhampton to cross the plain which I shan't do for many months yet it seems. I am a lecturer now – delivered a lecture on scales last week & didn't perish with the effort.

        Yours ever
        Edward Thomas

260

Written in pencil.
Thomas explains the delay in his promotion.

                        [in pencil, ?early 1916]

There was some bad luck in my trouble. I counted on the other man being in within a few minutes. He wasn't till next morning. So I suffered for bad judgment & appearing to conspire with him to break the law.

Do you ever see anyone now? I heard from Garnett the other day but with no news. He wanted to know if anything was being done about the Civil List. He didn't know if Hudson had done anything nor do I. I only know he is still in hospital.

I wish you could come down on Sunday; get here at 12.30 – I mean to Gidea Park Station.
I could meet you.

> Yours ever
> E.T.

261

Written in pencil.
In a 11 February 1916 letter to Bottomley, Thomas writes "De la Mare continues to wear himself out at reviewing and making more money than he really needs."

> 13 Rusham Rd
> 9 February 1916

My dear Mrs de la Mare,

I should like a cake very much or a gingerbread by Jinnie, & camp is certainly the place to send it to. The only reason I did not return there on Sunday was that I somehow took a bad chill which hasn't improved much yet. It is better to be laid up here than in camp, I suppose, though I can't imagine anything more tiring & boring than this. And the fine weather makes it worse. I should like to be at Steep or Netherhampton. What a pity Jack hasn't found a way of resting as I have done these seven months.

I doubt if I shall get out before the end of this week★ so it would be best to let the cake keep till then — I think the older a home made cake is, the nicer it is. It is an age since I saw you & I am afraid another age may pass before I can come again. Give my love to Jinnie, please, & Colin, & Dick, & Florence.

> Yours most sincerely
> Edward Thomas

★or beginning of next

262

Written in pencil, this unsigned letter is creased and hard to read.
Bottomley showed Thomas's poems to Lascelles Abercrombie and R.C. Trevelyan. Impressed, they agreed to include eighteen in An Annual of New

Poetry, *which contained none of de la Mare's poems.*
*De la Mare reviewed the poems of Maurice Hewlett, a successful historical
novelist and friend of his, in the May 1909* Bookman.

From P.E. Thomas 4229
D. Coy
Artists Rifles
Hut 15
Hare Hall Camp
Romford
25 February 1916

My dear de la Mare,

I am all right now thanks. I have been back 10 days & doing the
ordinary work. It would have been a great pleasure to see you but
as soon as I could get out I went home. From what you told me I
knew it was useless trying to see you on my way back. I brought a
cake with me. But I am sure the one Jinny made will have
improved in the interval. I shall be delighted to have it. As to
tobacco, a mild cake tobacco takes least room, but I usually smoke
York River. It is the cheapest good tobacco & a most ancient
friend.

Yes it seems as if I shall crop up in the annual. I havent made
the choice yet. It will [amusing?] them Frost may be one of us. I
do hope you will. Constables are to Stereotype all contributions
with a view to reprinting in separate volumes if they want to. They
will want to reprint you. That's plain.

I wish I could get to Stone Henge & Broad Chalk. I remember
Hewlett's house. Stone Henge was the only thing in the world
apparently when I saw it first, except evening sky after rain. But I
have seen it rather as you did, with the barbed wire & the police-
man's box conspicuous.

263

Written in pencil.
In the introduction to The Eighteen Eighties: Essays by Fellows of the
Royal Society of Literature, *1930, de la Mare records his "early infatuation"
for Pater, "much less […] on account of what he said […] than on account of
his seductive, his very unusual way of saying it. He breathed an incantation,
and from incantation one is apt to waken more coldly disillusioned than is
quite fair to the enchanter."*

Hut 15
Tuesday
[in pencil, ?early 1916]

My dear de la Mare,

Your letter came on Sunday & your parcels on Monday. They cheered rather desolate days. The cakes are good. The tobacco is good. The chocolate I am sure, is good. It is more like a holiday than ever when a parcel like this – & more like being at school. I am half schoolmaster & half boy now. Six lectures a week, & each of the six in any one week all the same. So the War Office now orders it. We shall hardly get out at all. Thus we give six courses of nine lectures in 9 weeks. But we may be shunted elsewhere at present 4 of us are instructing simply our own company, its 6 platoons. Some of us may go to other companies. I rather hope so, because although we should be split up, there would be more chance of promotion. We are more tied down & dependent than ever. As for leave, I can't see when I can reach Anerley or anywhere but home. I must go home because Helen finds the perpetual housework & increased solitude a good deal to bear.

It is a pity this is so unlikely a time for me to get charity from the Civil List, because I can hardly expect a time when I shall need it more. The next 4 years must be if not the worst still the most difficult, other things being equal. Suppose the war ended before this year is out, & suppose I were soon discharged, I couldn't begin to earn my own living by the ordinary means & I can't yet feel I might become a lecturer. As a matter of fact I expect I shall try the States. But I shall not build any hopes on the chance of a pension!

I don't know at all what Garnett has done or will do. The address is

19 Pond Place
    Chelsea S.W.

How wretched for you all to have whooping cough in the house. I hope they will soon get past the bed stage & enjoy it as a holiday. If I can enjoy this as a holiday I am sure Jinnie can enjoy whooping cough after a time. Still I don't expect you to enjoy split infinitives (or as Davies says the infinitive split) except when you discover them in Walter Pater — though I believe I could[.] Can't you come down some Sunday as for example next Sunday? The weather looks nearer Spring & this country is most pleasant till the

weekend crowds begin. With my love to you & your wife & all
Ever yours
Edward Thomas

264

Written in pencil.
It is interesting Thomas mentions Davies as his review of Davies's Child
Lovers and other poems *appears in the August 1916* Bookman. *He criticizes
an occasional tendency to be "a shade too explicit" but praises its joyful sincer-
ity: "we feel so often what he says in 'April's Charms' that he can taste joy."*
*When de la Mare won the 1911 Polignac Prize, he wanted to give Thomas a
present. Thomas asked for a rocking chair. See the letter Thomas wrote to de la
Mare at the end of November 1911.*
*Thomas's 'Home' ("Fair was the morning") records one of his outdoor work
trips at camp. It was composed on 7 and 10 March.*

Hut 3
Hare Hall Camp
Wednesday
[in pencil, probably March, early 1916]

My dear de la Mare,

It was very nice of you to send that rocking chair. I really ought
to send it back & see if I can go on buying matches & going to
cinemas after the new tax. But I will wait & convert it into
something more useful in this life. Thank you, I will forgive you
too – this time.

There is no news. I can't get leave, haven't been home for a
month & have no prospect of going. I work very hard, almost
entirely lecturing, & therefore indoors. It was pure luck that this
fine weather came at a time when we had work to do that had to
be done out of doors. They have at last made me a full corporal.

I wish your news were no worse than mine. You aren't fit
yourself & the children are still whooping. It is too bad. Pity you
aren't 40 & in Hare Hill camp – I mean you: I don't want Jinnie to
be 40.

I was wondering what was happening, if you had met Garnett
yet. Hudson, I take it, is too unwell, though he still writes a letter
that is a letter.

You won't come down then. John Freeman talks of coming this

Sunday, unless leave falls from the sky I wish you could come some time, on a Wednesday afternoon for instance, which is usually free from 1 onwards.

Do you hear from Hodgson now? I haven't run into him yet, though I heard he was in the county. Hooton, I gather, is out of work & no better in health. Davies I never see or hear of. Write again. Give my love to your wife & all of them.   Yours ever   E.T.

265

Thomas's application to the Civil List.
Edmund Gosse is a poet, author and critic, as well as Sunday Times *correspondent.*
John Galsworthy, a member of the Square Club, novelist and playwright.

Hut 3
Hare Hall Camp
16 April 1916

My dear de la Mare,

Your letter came with one from Garnett on Friday. Thank you. I am asking Garnett to suggest which books I ought to send & when he answers I will make up my mind. My choice is

Jefferies
'Borrow' or 'Swinburne'
'Four & Twenty Blackbirds' or 'Rest & Unrest'.

What do you think? Also, shall I try to get Lloyd George on my side later on? I don't know who else, besides Conrad & Hudson, would write. Gosse & Galsworthy occur to me. Would Newbolt?

There is still no leave to be had except on special grounds, but I hope to see you before long & to find the children unable to whoop. They should have some fine days on the coast. Here we are finding nests & expecting the cuckoo.

Yours ever
Edward Thomas.

266

Written in pencil.
Marsh is Edward Marsh.
Thomas wrote the four poems to his children and his wife between 29 March
to 9 April at Hare Hall camp.
De la Mare's 'The Riddlers', The Sunken Garden and Other Poems, 1917,
carries an echo of Thomas's 'If I were to Own'.

> Hut 3
> Hare Hall Camp
> Romsford
> 19 April 1916

I have asked Jones & Evans to send you copies of
> Jefferies
> Swinburne
> Rest & Unrest
> The South Country.

It was Garnett's choice & I could not choose alone. I take it you
will send them to Marsh or wherever they are to go. I have got
leave from tomorrow till Saturday. Just time to see the children.
> E.T.

267

Evidence of de la Mare's efforts in obtaining support for a Civil List Pension
for Thomas.

Confidential

> 17, Hanover Terrace,
> Regent's Park, N.W.
> 20 April 1916

My dear de la Mare
    I shall be happy to speak to the Prime Minister, (at a more
convenient season than now at the height of the crisis!) on the
claims of Mr Thomas. I would, however, gently venture to warn
you against the dangers of exaggerated language, which does more
to harm than to help a candidate. I have not see much of Mr

Thomas' writing, which is often creditable, but I have met with little of his that deserved the epithets 'rare' and 'beautiful.' He wrote a monograph on Swinburne which was certainly neither the one nor the other!

Unless Mr Thomas has debts, I cannot think the moment well chosen for an appeal to the King's bounty for him. He is a private, I suppose, in the Army, and his wife and children have therefore for the present some provision. I should have thought it would have been better to wait until peace was declared, when he would perhaps be in need of a special help before resuming his literary work. About this, you might furnish me with further information before I speak to the P.M.

> With kindest regard I am always sincerely [your?]
> Edmund Gosse

268

Written in pencil.
Ll. G. is Lloyd George
In a 13 May 1916 letter to Bottomley, Thomas writes "De la Mare came down for a Sunday a fortnight ago and spoke tentatively. He mostly does now. He isn't well and might be perplexed in the extreme. He doesn't always write as well as he used to. But his verses I hardly ever see."

> Hut 3 Thursday
> [postmarked 27 AP 16]

What about Sunday? If you can come let me know your train — one not before 11.30 — & write soon in case the post is slow. We can get a walk then.

I hope the books arrived.

Ll. G. is being approached.

I haven't heard who is writing the letter.

> E.T.

Garnett didn't think '24 Blackbirds' would weigh with ministers.

269

Thomas did not secure a pension but received £300 from the Royal Literary Fund.
The Artillery carried with it a larger pension for widows but also increased risk.

Y.M.C.A.
With H. M. Forces on Active Service

Hut 14
Wednesday
in pencil, 31 May ? 7 June 1916]

My dear de la Mare,

Thank you for sending me the news & for bringing it about. As I was not expecting anything it was really good news, especially as it came so soon. I will write to Marsh about it. It should last another 2 years & help me to do something for Mervyn. It does remove immediate anxiety. Thank you again & I will spend some of it coming to Anerley when I have a chance. Will you address this letter to Marsh?

My love to you all
Ever yours
ET.

No news. I put my name down for an artillery commission but heard this morning that they would not recommend me without a knowledge of higher mathematics. This I could soon acquire. The only thing is one needs influence — to get a colonel to ask for me. I must not offer myself. You don't know an artillery colonel who might help?

270

Written in pencil.
R.A. Scott-James, editor of New Weekly *before the war, is now in the army.*
Thomas and de la Mare lodged at Dillybrook farm near Bath in order to write in 1913.
De la Mare's trip was to America to give a lecture in Rupert Brooke's place and to accept the Yale University Howland Prize, awarded posthumously to

Brooke for his 1914 and Other Poems.
Harley Granville Barker, actor, director, critic and playwright, served in the Red Cross during the war.

Royal Artillery School
Trowbridge
Thursday 28 September 1916

My dear de la Mare,

I couldn't question Scott James because he was away with an injured foot & I didn't know his address. After all, I did pass the exam. I came here a week ago & am now fairly settled, as far as it is possible to be, in tents. The work is very hard & by 7.30 when it ends I have not really mastered the work of the day. Levers & pulleys & c are not in my line, I find. But we had some lovely days & nights & things are not as unpleasant as we were told. I had leave on gratuity to go over to Dillybrook. They asked after you. The old man is dead – died suddenly a year ago. His heart was bad.

Are your plans settling yet? If people look after you you ought to do well by the trip. I wish I was going, if I didn't wish I was going somewhere else. The latest rumour is that the men over 35 may be put on coast defence, which I hope is not true. I suppose the coast has to be defended, but I would rather not be shelved at this time of day.

We are not moving till Oct. 9. Our address then will be Paul's Nursery, High Beech, Loughton, Essex.

Granville Barker is here & held in awe except by the Sergeant Major, possibly by him. I have not run into him yet.

Well, if I don't go to Weymouth for the very elaborate training for coast defence, I shall probably be here well into November. With short weekends it will be impossible in either case to see you, I am afraid. But I hope you are going to have a safe & lovely time. My love to them all

Yours ever
Edward Thomas
still cadet P.E.T.

271

Thomas writes to Frost on 4 November 1916 of de la Mare 'I hope you will see him. It is sometime since I saw him. We rather fence with one another now,

remembering we once got on very well.'
Although Frost and de la Mare did meet in America, Frost expresses his ambivalence about such a meeting in a 14 November 1916 letter to Louis Untermeyer, fearing that de la Mare 'scorns America and has only come over for what he can get out of us'.

> Royal Artillery Barracks
> Trowbridge
> Wiltshire
> 29 October 1916

My dear de la Mare,

I wish you luck & some surprises – for I don't suppose you expect anything very pleasant – & I hope you won't have to dive for them. I should like to be coming too. As I can't, give my love to Frost if you find you can see him. He is at Franconia, New Hampshire, but would come a long way to see you. Before you return I ought to be somewhere out of England. You never know. I think I would sooner go East than just to Flanders. I ought to have a commission next month, having passed my exams so far. I am only 4 or 5 from the bottom in a squad of 42, so I feel no great assurance yet. The great thing is not to hit your friends, & you are perhaps as well out of the danger zone. I wonder where Hodgson is? I suppose either in Anti-Aircraft or Coast Defence. I hope I shall be prevented from Coast Defence. I want a far greater change than I have had so far. Goodbye. Give my love to your wife & all.

> Yours ever
> (Cadet) Edward Thomas.

272

Written in pencil.
Thomas's praise of Peacock Pie *echoes his comment in the September 1913* Bookman *where he writes "nobody else can mingle so variously jollity with magic as Mr. de la Mare does."*

> 244 Siege Battery
> ~~Artillery Mobilization Camp~~

15 Camp
Codford
nr Salisbury
12 January 1917

My dear Mrs de la Mare,

This is to say goodbye, which I was not able to do in any other way. We are here for a week or so before going out – I suppose to France. I want you to give my love to Jack and the children. When I was at home on my last leave Bronwen & Bab[a] were full of 'Peacock Pie', & I wish Jack knew how much they liked to hear it read through. I don't know any poet who could give such perfect pleasure. Good bye.

Yours ever
(2nd Lt.) Edward Thomas

273

Written in pencil, with PS in ink.
De la Mare found himself in great demand in America to give lectures, and journal requests for poems multiplied, so he delayed his return till February, too late to see Thomas.

24 Siege Battery
15 Camp
Codford
22 January 1917

My dear Mrs de la Mare,

I went over to see Lady Newbolt & Mrs Furse on Sunday. They were very kind, but I own I enjoyed most feeling quite near to Jack for a time. It seems impossible for me to see him. I may go any day after Wednesday or before today week. It depends on whether I go in charge of an advance party or not. But in any case I can't get away again, except as far as I can walk on a Sunday.

I will keep this note open till I know for certain. Goodbye. My address will be 244 Siege Battery, B.E.F. France.

Yours ever
Edward Thomas

Later

We shall have left by Monday. I personally might go before, but I don't think so. I would go again to the Newbolts, but I can't walk much at the moment, & the trains are inconvenient.

Please give my love to Jack & the children.

274

Written in pencil.
De la Mare's The Sunken Garden and Other Poems *appeared in a limited edition in 1917.*
Thomas took a copy of Shakespeare's sonnets with him to the Front.
He wrote no poems but kept a diary.

February 14

My dear de la Mare,

I was sorry not to see you again before I left. It was something like seeing you when I went over to Netherhampton. I meant to have gone again but we left too soon. We have been nearly three weeks over here & we crawled slowly & uncomfortably up country & have now been some days in our position or near it. We are billeted in a farm 2 or 3 miles back in hilly country. We are preparing our positions, meantime firing with another battery's guns. Personally my most interesting work has been going round the trenches examining observation posts & seeing what can be seen from them. I have been within about 500 yards of the Hun & only too well within range of his trench mortars & machine guns. I have enjoyed it very much though 15 miles in the trenches equals twice as much in open country. The risk is rather stimulating, but is not very great because the job takes the mind off other things for the most part. We have had glorious clear cold weather & I have enjoyed it except sometimes at night, because we have slept rather rough. The worst thing has been not receiving a single letter from England. Nobody has. It takes a long time before a unit begins to get letters regularly. So I have no idea what has been happening for these three weeks. Are you back? Have you a book to come? I believe I could read it here. I read nothing so far except a few of the sonnets at times. Of course I can't write, but then I don't want to or think about it.

We are rather comfortable now, but we don't all enjoy the gramophone equally when it sings 'Where does daddy go when he goes out' or 'Wait till I'm as old as father.' But we are a fairly harmonious party in a way, with the help of a great deal of nonsense. The man who loves the [?] is a ranker, who has been in the army since he was a boy, a perfect type of the old army, merry, careless, & kind, who talks entirely in comic proverbs, clichés, & snaps of music hall songs & low stories – the one man who knows his job through & through. He & I get on excellently somehow.

Give my love to your wife & the children & to Hodgson if ever you see him.

Yours ever
Edward Thomas
Do write to me as
2/Lt P E Thomas, 244 Seige Battery, B.E F. France.

275

Written in purple pencil.
De la Mare spent a night at Frost's house in Amherst during his last circuit of readings and lectures in America.
De la Mare's friend, the illustrator Lovat Fraser, who worked on drawings for Peacock Pie, *married the American actress Grace Inez Crawford in February 1917.*
Frost's Mountain Interval *was published in November 1916.*
Thomas's Poems, 1917 *came out after his death.*

March 9

My dear de la Mare, I expect you had a letter from me soon after you wrote. At least I posted one about 3 weeks ago. Letters take a long while coming, always a week. I will write to you now in case I have less time or no time later, which is very possible. I am just moving back to my Battery after nearly 3 weeks at a Heavy Artillery Group headquarters, which has been rather an idle time but has shown me quite as much as I want to see of the way things are run. It has been idle but not exactly snug as we are only 2400 yards from the Hun & in a city which he shells daily. I think I shall prefer being shelled in a position where we are doing something direct in retaliation & not just map work. We are in a big rather pretentious modern house with only one shell hole in it. The town hall & cathedral are all holes. It is cold, because it is big & because fuel is very scarce. I shiver all day indoors, but luckily what work I do is often out of doors & though I can't f<u>ee</u>l that my chances of escape are very good I contrive to enjoy many things. I think I enjoy the people best of all. But that may be cleared up when the Z arrives, whenever that is to be. The battery is in an orchard outside the town. We may see the apple blossom, but I doubt that. Nobody is very hopeful. I think myself that things may go on at this rate for more than a year. The rate may be changed, but not if the Hun can help it, & his retirement looks very inconvenient in every way.

I wish you had said more about Frost. One is absolutely friend-less here. Everybody has something to conceal & he does so by pretending to be like everybody else. All the talk is shop or worse. It is all tedious & uncomfortable except at odd moments. But then so is life anywhere, I suppose. It is all very different from the newspapers, & very much like what one would expect. Cold, dirt, fatigue, uncertainty, & the accidental beautiful or amusing thing. If only one wasn't taught to think it was something else. But then this is the case everywhere, not only out here.

I heard Lovat Fraser was married, bu[t] did not hear to whom, though I understood that was interesting. Hodgson I have heard nothing of. Hooton wrote me a jocular letter the other day which did not make me feel jocular. A machine gun up the street is hammering away at nails for coffins but I never see the dead in more than a canvas bag. There is 'some stuff coming in' this after-noon — i.e. some enemy shells are falling in the streets. It is snowing & dull, or there would be still more firing. What there is must be blind – without observation I have not met any one I know out here. You say it would be good if we could have a talk, but, you know, I fancy it would not do to have a real friend out here. Intimacy & some introspection would be very much against the frame of mind that makes things at least [toler]able. Comradeship is the right thing, but I have tasted less of that than I expected.

There are so many times when one has really nothing to do & yet no freedom to do what one likes, even if there were anything one still liked beyond warmth & food & a clear head.

But don't take this very seriously. This life at headquarters has been too inactive for me & now a cold day waiting alone till my things are packed puts the lid on it. also I am a little anxious after being away from the guns for 3 weeks, half my time out here.

Send me your poems whenever they come, & I hope it will be soon. I found Frost's 'Mountain Interval' here & every day I read a sonnet or two. My own verses should be out soon. I wonder what will come of them. Give my love to your wife – & I hope she is better now you are back – & to all the children.   Yours ever

Edward Thomas.

276

After Thomas's death, de la Mare petitioned for help for Helen Thomas.

Dear Mr

The Prime Minister will be shortly approached by Captain Morgan & Sir Alfred [Maud?] with a petition that the widow of the late Edward Thomas should be granted a Civil List Pension. But it is necessary that their hands should be strengthened by letters in support from literary men. Will you, as a particular admirer of the high literary qualities of Thomas's work, send me a letter expressing your cordial sympathy with our object together with a few lines of warm tribute?

Sincerely yours

W de l M.

[~~that~~ & them I have been asked to ~~write this~~ to obtain]

277

A reply to de la Mare's request for support for Thomas's wife.
E. G. is Edmund Gosse.

I'm sending you my poor little letter. I trust you will have many letters. I only wish someone could whisper a word of caution in the Prime Minister's ear when the petition is presented – "You see he was a Welshman, & you will be particularly careful & probably leave the question to be decided on its merits by some great literary expert. And that would be quite right only please don't let it be E.G."

278

After Thomas's death, de la Mare continued his efforts to help Helen Thomas.

KINGS LAND,
SHIPLEY,
HORSHAM.
7 May 1917

Dear Mr. de la Mare,

 I enclose you my letter with regard to the Petition for the Civil List Pension for Mrs. Thomas, and I am,

Very faithfully yours,
H Belloc.

From Thomas's 'The Stile' in *Light and Twilight*, 1911

One day I stopped by the stile at the corner to say good-bye to a friend who had walked thus far with me. It was about half an hour after the sunset of a dry, hot day among the many wet ones in that July. We had been talking easily and warmly together, in such a way that there was no knowing whose was any one thought, because we were in electrical contact and each leapt to complete the other's words, just as if some poet had chosen to use the form of an eclogue and had made us the two shepherds who were to utter his mind through our dialogue. When he spoke I had already the same thing in the same words to express. When either of us spoke we were saying what we could not have said to any other man at any other time.

But as we reached the stile our tongues and our steps ceased together, and I was instantly aware of the silence through which our walking and talking had drawn a thin line up to this point.

Thomas's 'The sun used to shine'

composed Hare Hall, 22 May 1916

The sun used to shine while we two walked
Slowly together, paused and started
Again, and sometimes mused, sometimes talked
As either pleased, and cheerfully parted

Each night. We never disagreed
Which gate to rest on. The to be
And the late past we gave small heed.
We turned from men or poetry

To rumours of the war remote
Only till both stood disinclined
For aught but the yellow flavorous coat
Of an apple wasps had undermined;

Or a sentry of dark betonies,
The stateliest of small flowers on earth,
At the forest verge; or crocuses
Pale purple as if they had their birth

In sunless Hades fields. The war
Came back to mind with the moonrise
Which soldiers in the east afar
Beheld then. Nevertheless, our eyes

Could as well imagine the Crusades
Or Caesar's battles. Everything
To faintness like those rumours fades –
Like the brook's water glittering

Under the moonlight – like those walks
Now – like us two that took them, and
The fallen apples, all the talks
And silences – like memory's sand

When the tide covers it late or soon,
And other men through other flowers
In those fields under the same moon
Go talking and have easy hours.

Select bibliography

Manuscripts and websites

Bodleian Library, Letters to Walter de la Mare, MS Eng lett c 376
Edward Thomas Fellowship, www.edward-thomas-fellowship.org.uk
First World War Poetry Digital Archive, www.oucs.ox.ac.uk/ww1lit/collection/thomas
Walter de la Mare Society, www.walterdelamare.co.uk

Walter de la Mare's Writing

The Complete Poems of Walter de la Mare (London: Faber, 1969; revised, 1975)
Edward Thomas: Collected Poems with foreword by Walter de la Mare in the appendix (London: Faber and Faber, 2004)
Short Stories 1895-1926 (London: Giles de la Mare, 1996)
Short Stories 1927-1952 (London: Giles de la Mare, 2001)
The Return (London: Arnold, 1910)
The Three Mulla-Mulgars (London: Duckworth, 1910)

Edward Thomas's Writing

A language not to be betrayed: selected prose of Edward Thomas, ed. Edna Longley (Manchester: Carcanet Press, 1981)
Celtic Stories (Oxford: Clarendon Press, 1911)
The Childhood of Edward Thomas: a fragment of autobiography (London: Faber and Faber, 1938)
Cloud Castle and other Papers (London: Duckworth, 1922)
Edward Thomas on the Georgians, ed. Richard Emeny (Cheltenham: Cyder Press, 2004)
Edward Thomas's Poets, ed. Judy Kendall (Manchester: Carcanet, 2007)
Edward Thomas: The Annotated Collected Poems, ed. Edna Longley (Newcastle: Bloodaxe Books, 2008)
Feminine Influence on the Poets (London: Martin Secker, 1910)
The Happy-go-lucky Morgans (London: Duckworth, 1913)
The Last Sheaf (London: Jonathan Cape, 1928)
Letters from Edward Thomas to Gordon Bottomley, ed. R.G. Thomas (London: Oxford University Press, 1968)
Light and Twilight (London: Duckworth, 1911; repr. Holt: Laurel Books, 2000)

Rest and Unrest (London: Duckworth, 1910)

Secondary Material

Croft, P. J., *Autograph Poetry in the English Language* (London: Cassell, 1973), vol. 2, p. 161.
Emeny, Richard, ed., *Edward Thomas 1878-1917: Towards a complete checklist of his publications* (Blackburn: White Sheep Press, 2004)
Thomas, R.G., *Edward Thomas: A Portrait* (Oxford: Clarendon Press, 1985)
Whistler, Theresa, *The Life of Walter de la Mare: Imagination of the Heart* (London: Duckworth, 1993)

Articles

Bottomley, Gordon, 'A Note on Edward Thomas', *Welsh Review*, 4.3 (September 1945), 166-76
Kendall, Judy, ' 'A Poet At Last'; William H. Davies and Edward Thomas', *Almanac:Yearbook of Welsh Writing in English* ed. Katie Gramich (Cardigan: Parthian, 2008), pp. 32-54
Kendall, Judy, 'A Tale of Two Poets: Walter de la Mare and Edward Thomas The Bodleian Correspondence', *Walter de la Mare Society Magazine*, 10, January 2007, 24-29
Woolf, Virginia, 'Flumina Amem Silvasque', *Times Literary Supplement*, 11 October 1917, 489
Woolf, Virginia, 'A Lesson from the East' *Times Literary Supplement*, 30 May 1918, 253

Appendix: Guide to Folio Numbers

Section I 1906-1910

Letters	Folios
1-11	1-11
12	12-13
13	14-15
14	16-17
15-17	18 –20
18	21-22
19	23
20	24
21	25-26
22-25	27-30
26	31-32
27-35	33-41
36	304-305
37-43	42-48
44	318
45-47	49-51
48	53-54
49-51	55-57
52	52
53-57	58-62
58	63-64
59-80	64-85
81	86-7
82 -87	88-93
88	94-95

Section II 1910-1913

Letters	Folios
89-91	96-98
92	99-102
93	103
94	104-106
95-96	107-108
97	302
98-103	109-114
104	115-116
105-108	117-120
109	121-122
110-115	123-128

Letters	Folios
116	131
117-118	129-130
119-120	132-133
121	134-135
122	136
123	137-138
124-125	139-140
126-127	142-143
128	144-145
129-130	146-147
131	141
132-135	148-151
136	307
137-141	152-156
142	308-309
143-145	157-159
146	168
147-148	160-161
149	162-163
150-153	164-167
154-155	169-170
156	303
157	171
158	172-173
159-161	174-176
162-163	179-180
164	181-182
165-172	183-190
173	191-192
174-176	193-195
177	196-197
178	198
179	200
180	199
181	201
182	306
183	202-203

Section III 1913-1917

Letters	Folios
184	204
185	216
186	205
187	220-221

Letters	Folios
188-190	206-208
191	209-210
192-196	211-215
197	217-218
198	219
199	222
200	177-178
201	223-224
202-211	225-234
212	314
213-221	235-243
226	310-311
227	247
228	248-249
223	244
222	315
224-225	245-246
229-232	250-253
233	254
234-239	255-260
240	261-262
241-243	264-266
244	263
245-247	267-269
248-249	272-273
250	317
251-253	274-276
254	270-271
255-262	277-284
263	285-286
264	287-288
265-266	289-290
267	319-320
276-277	321-322
268-269	291-292
270	293-294
271-273	295-297
274	298-299
275	300-301
278	323

Undated folios

	312-313
	316

Acknowledgements

Special thanks to Colin Harris and the staff of Oxford University Bodleian Special Collections Reading Rooms; also thanks for use of their resources to the Oxford Bodleian Library, Cambridge University Library, British Library Newspapers Collection, John Rylands Library and Manchester Metropolitan Library. The practical support of the late David and Diana Kendall, Bridget Kendall, Eleanor Kercher and Alex Lipinski on visits to these institutions was essential to the completion of this work.

Thanks also to Alan Brown, Michael Schmidt, Stephen Stuart-Smith and the late Peter Widdowson for initial encouragement; the British Academy for a grant to fund the transcription process; the University of Salford for practical support; Frances Guthrie and Giles de la Mare of the Walter de la Mare Society; Richard Emeny, Anne Harvey and Colin Thornton of the Edward Thomas Fellowship; Lorna Beckett of the Rupert Brooke Society; Jean Moorcroft Wilson for help in dating some of the letters; and Mick Felton of Seren Books for seeing the book through to completion.

I am grateful to the Edward Thomas Estate for permission to use unpublished and published material on and by Edward Thomas; the Literary Trustees of Walter de la Mare and The Society of Authors as their representative for permission to reprint Walter de la Mare's 'Longlegs' from *Peacock Pie* and *Down-Adown-Derry* and 'There once was an old, old woman' from the *New Stateman;* the Bodleian Library, University of Oxford, owners of Letters to Walter de la Mare (Eng lett 376), for permission to use Thomas's unpublished letters to de la Mare; and the Kendall family for permission to use the unpublished poem 'A Seventeenth Century Icon' by the late David Kendall, held in copyright by the estate of David George Kendall.

Particular thanks are due to Piers Pennington of Corpus Christi College, Oxford, for assiduous transcription of the letters and assistance in the editing process, and observation of several features in the letters, such as the judicious positioning of the watermark in letter 110 (folio 123).

Index

A Note on the Editor

Judy Kendall was born in Oxford, grew up in Cambridge and has spent a third of her working life in township schools in Harare, Zimbabwe, and a national university in Kanazawa, Japan. Currently a senior lecturer in English and Creative Writing at Salford University, she has worked in music and travel journalism, community and development education, prisons and schools. She is a scholar on Edward Thomas and her books on him include *Edward Thomas: the Origins of his Poetry* (2012) and *Edward Thomas's Poets* (2007).

Kendal also writes creatively in the areas of poetry, short fiction and visual text. She also has a background in writing for the theatre. A Hawthornden fellow, she has won several national and international awards for her plays, poetry and short fiction. She has completed co-translation projects from Japanese to English and is active in haiku and renga related creative work: www.white-peak-darkpeak.co.uk. She has also co-translated poetry from Friesian, German and Hungarian. Her latest poetry collection is *Climbing Postcards* (2012).